GPS

FOR OUR SOULS:

A to Z COORDINATES TO ENLIGHTENMENT

By **Victor M. Parachin**

Library of Congress Cataloging-in-Publication Data

Parachin, Victor M.
  GPS for our souls : A to Z coordinates to enlightenment / by
Victor M. Parachin. -- 1st [edition].
     pages cm
  Includes bibliographical references and index.
  ISBN 978-0-8283-2576-9 (paerback : alk. paper) 1.
Spiritual life. 2. Spiritual life--Buddhism. 3. Asia--Religion.
4. Philosophy, Asian. 5. Wisdom--Religious aspects. 6.
Bodhisattva (The concept) I. Title.

   BL624.P2878 2015
   204'.2--dc23

                              2015018982

Paperback ISBN 9780828325769
E-Book ISBN 9780828335776

Branden Books
PO Box 812094
Wellesley MA 02482

www.brandenbooks.com

INTRODUCTION

en.light.en.ment / Noun

1.   The state of being enlightened

2.   The act of enlightening

In Buddhist thought there is a word for a person like you and that word is:

Bodhisattva.

A Bodhisattva is any individual who is committed to achieving his or her enlightenment in order help others become enlightened. The Buddha taught: "The greatest gift is to give people your enlightenment, to share it. It has to be the greatest."

This book – *GPS For Our Souls* - is a tool for you to use on your journey toward enlightenment. It can be helpful to remember that enlightenment is always the result of an intentional journey and that enlightenment generally comes gradually and in moments. The Sufi sage who was born in India, Indries Shah, (1924-1996) rightly observed: "Enlightenment must come little by little - otherwise it would overwhelm."

In addition, Joseph Campbell, mythologist and author, offers this insight: "Enlightenment, cannot be communicated, but only

the way to enlightenment."
GPS For Our Souls contains stories, quotes and lessons of Eastern wisdom which point the way toward enlightenment. Rather than chapters, this book is arranged according to the letters of the alphabet with some letters containing more than one entry.

Victor M. Parachin

A

ATTENTION

PAY ATTENTION TO YOUR LIFE.

The greatest appointment you have in life is with yourself.
Be sure to show up on time and pay attention.
Laura Teresa Marquez

In ancient China the people of a small village received a
command from the regional governor to build a shrine for the
emperor. They were given a deadline with the promise of a
sizeable reward if the deadline was met. Immediately they
scouted out and chose a location for the shrine. Although the
site was ideal, it had one drawback: it contained a dry well
which had been abandoned years earlier. Before they could
begin with construction of the shrine, the well had to be filled
so they brought in a donkey to transport piles of pebbles,
sand and mud.

After only a few days of work, an accident took place. The
donkey was led too closely to the exposed well, lost his
footing and fell into the deep well. The villagers tried to lift
the creature out but were unsuccessful. After many failed
attempts they gave up. It was simply going to take too long to
rescue him and they were, after all, on a deadline.
Reluctantly, they decided to sacrifice the donkey. Using only
human labor, they proceeded to haul rock, sand and mud to

the well. There they shoveled pebbles, sand and mud into the well assuming the animal would simply be buried alive. As the pebbles, sand, and mud fell on the donkey, he realized what was happening and began to wail in protest. Though the villagers heard the creature crying out, they ignored the pleas. The value of one animal was far less than the reward they would receive for meeting the deadline. They continued to shovel.

After a while, the donkey stopped wailing. The villagers wondered about the silence thinking to themselves: *Is the donkey dead already? Has he given up protesting? Why the abrupt silence?* Out of curiosity, they peered into the well and a surprising sight greeted them. The donkey was alive and active. As the pebbles, sand and mud rained down on him, he shrugged them off, stamped on them until they were tightly packed below his feet. This provided him with a solid base of ground which lifted him a bit higher each time. Before long, the donkey got high enough inside the well and with one powerful leap, jumped out. Amazed, the villagers watched the creature with new respect as he trotted off with his head held high.

Connect that story to the quotation from Laura Teresa Marques: *The greatest appointment you have in life is with yourself. Be sure to show up on time and pay attention.* There are many times in life when we have the experience of the donkey. We're trapped in a deep, dark well and debris is dropping upon us. Like the donkey we can wail, protest, and curse our condition. Sadly that's all some people do in such circumstances. However, the donkey quickly realized that wailing, protesting, and cursing were of no help. Instead, he chose to pay attention to what was happening. The creature was able to set aside that cycle of negativity. In so doing, he freed his mind to respond more creatively and resourcefully.

Like the donkey, when we pay attention to life we become more aware of what is really happening and intuitively know exactly what is needed for our good. And, like the donkey, we can make use of the negative. Just as the donkey used the pebbles, sand and mud as building blocks, we can use negative events and issues which come our way as the raw materials on which to build an even stronger foundation. Some ways to do that include:

When we face a life threatening illness. Rather than despair we can seek out the best possible care medically; we can seek out the best possible support from family and friends; we can seek to cultivate spiritual disciplines for managing the illness and feelings connected to it.

When we experience a relationship breakup. Rather than become bitter over this we can choose to become better; looking back to see what went wrong, our role in the breakup and moving forward as a healthier, stronger person.

When we are under intense criticism. Rather than cringe or react to it, we can listen to it with patience and maturity. If there is truth in the criticism, we can change and grow. If there's no truth in it, we can work to shrug it off.

When we are dealing with a major life challenge. Rather than run from it, we can face it directly and creatively find methods to downsize the challenge and eventually triumph over it.

When we are gossiped about. Rather than be leveled by false rumors, we can choose to live in such a way that others will be unable to believe the gossip.

When someone we love has died. Rather than live with continuous depression and despair, we can choose to find light and hope in this dark time.

Remember the lesson from the donkey: *When we pay attention we become fully engaged with life and awake to all the possibilities present.*

AWARENESS

SIGHT VERSUS INSIGHT

> Barn's burnt down.
> Now, I can see the moon.
> **Masahide**

Those words were written by Masahide (1657-1723), a Samurai poet who also practiced medicine in Japan. He wrote this poem in 1688 shortly after his house, barn and everything he owned was burned up. Though he wrote many poems, this one about the barn and moon is most remembered and most famous.

An alternate translation of his words reads this way:

> Since my house burned down;
> now I own a better view
> of the rising moon.

Ask yourself: "Why did this poem become his most famous? What is in it which makes itself attractive to people?"

Several answers are possible. First, there is the positive outlook in the presence of tragedy. A building is gone but now there is a better view of the beautiful moon. Secondly, there is some humor evident in Masahide - "The building was blocking my view." Thirdly, his words are an eloquent reminder that some people merely have sight while others have insight.

Another person in the same circumstances could simply weep and wring his hands in despair at the loss of so much property and goods. That person only sees what has been lost. The trick in life is to move from sight to insight, which is precisely what Masahide was able to do and, he did it promptly. Within a day or two after his building was devoured by flames, he expressed insight not merely sight.

There is an interesting modern parallel to Masahide's wisdom and it comes from the great inventor Thomas Edison. When he was 67 years of age in 1914, fire destroyed his plant. Ten buildings went up in flames. He was insured for $2 million but the losses were more than $7 million. Yet, as he watched the flames consume his life's work he spoke to reporters who were present telling them: "There is great value in this disaster. All our mistakes are burned up. Thank God we can start anew." Then he informed his 7,000 employees they would not be out of work but to report in the next day to do salvage work and begin rebuilding the plants.

This lesson from Masahide and Edison is one which any of us can apply to life whenever a loss, a disappointment or even a tragedy comes our way. We need to train our eyes not only to see what has been taken from us but what remains and what can emerge from the loss.

This is the difference between sight and insight.

B

BALANCE

LIVING A BALANCED LIFE

> People with great gifts are easy to find;
> but symmetrical and balanced ones never.
> **Ralph Waldo Emerson**

After his enlightenment, the Buddha was often criticized by other spiritual seekers. Their complaint: he was not longer living an austere lifestyle. He was eating nutritious meals and wearing a fine robe. They, on the other hand, dressed poorly, existed on a small meal of rice and often slept on a bed of nails. They considered his life far too comfortable for a spiritual teacher. So they said to him: "We don't understand what kind of teacher you are. You are soft, weak and indulgent."

Replying, the Buddha said: "I, too, have slept on nails; I've stood with my eyes open to the sun in the hot sands beside the Ganges. I've eaten so little food that you couldn't fill one fingernail with the amount I ate each day. Whatever ascetic practices any human being has done, I, also, have done them. Through them all I have learned that fighting against oneself through such practices is not the way." Then, the Buddha explained he was following middle way that balance between austerity and comfort, poverty and wealth, self-denial and self-indulgence. He likened the middle way to the playing of a lute. The strings had to be just right, not too tight and not too loose.

Based on the Buddha's life and experience, ask yourself: "How balanced is my life?" "What areas need adjustment for better balance to be present?" Then, take the appropriate steps today.

BHAKTI
CONSIDER THE PRACTICE OF BHAKTI YOGA

> Be Me-minded, devoted to Me, sacrifice to Me,
> do obedience to Me – thus you will come to Me.
> **Bhagavad Gita 18:65**

The word "bhakti" simply means devotion. There is a form of yoga called "bhakti yoga" or yoga of the heart. This practice does not involve doing yoga poses but rather opening the heart via devotion to a favored Divinity. Bhakti practice is something we in the west can and should engage in because it is soul expanding. Honor that Divinity via these kinds of activities:

Set up a small altar in your home with a favorite image or representation of that divinity. (a picture of the Virgin Mary, Jesus, a favored saint etc)

Meditate on the image you've chosen. Gaze at him/her.

Say a prayer before a meal expressing gratitude to the divine for the abundance of food you enjoy.

Practice humility. One good way to do this is by doing something no one else likes or wants to do. Make this your 'offering' to the Divinity.

Do the Jesuit "examination of conscience" by looking back over the last 24 hours of your life noticing where you sensed the Divine presence.

Set aside time for meditation – even briefly – each day of the week.

Practice forgiveness: for others and toward yourself.

Pray throughout the day expressing gratitude for the good things which come your way and gratitude for spiritual support you receive to deal with the hard issues of your day.

Serve others. Let such service be you way of honoring your Divinity.

Engage in ritual. Consider lighting a candle on your home altar every time you enter your home. As you light the candle, pause to say a brief prayer or spend a moment in silence.

These are ways of fanning the flame of love and respect you feel for a Divine figure. They will also keep you spiritually connected to that Divinity.

BREATH

TAKE A DEEP BREATH!

If you breathe well, you will live long on the earth.
Hindu Proverb

It's long been noted that most elderly Indian yogis exhibit athletic bodies and appearance that people half their age would love to have. Connected to this fact is the Eastern principle that life is measured in the number of breaths we take, not in the number of years we live. Furthermore, it has been observed that living creatures which breathe more slowly tend to live longer than those with rapid breathing rates. For example:

CREATUREBREATHS PER MINUTELIFESPAN average

Hare5510
Monkey30 15
Chicken3014
Dog2822
Cat2425
Horse1640
Human15-1870
Tortoise1-3190 +

The conclusion in Eastern philosophy is that breath control (called 'pranayama') prolongs life. Consequently, the breath and controlling it is a prime focus during times of meditation. Those who are skeptical find this way of looking at this more interesting: *whether or not pranayama adds years to life, it does add life to the years.*

The story of the Tortoise and the Hare may, in fact, be a lesson about pranayama. At the start, the hare rushed out taking the lead. Thought the normal breathing rate of a hare tends to be around 55 breaths per minute, it was certainly breathing more rapidly because of the effort it was exerting. Both running and rapid breathing wear the body out quickly, so the hare was forced to make frequent rest stops to rest and regain breath control. As a result of the erratic breathing pattern and stopping to rest, the hare eventually lost the race.

On the other hand, the tortoise, which takes 1-3 breaths per minute, started the race slowly managing to maintain his steady pace throughout. Because he walked normally and therefore maintained his normal breath pattern he completed the course without exhaustion, without having to stop for rest and won the race.

Here's a simple breath meditation exercise for you to experiment with. Sit comfortably, in a chair or cushion on the floor. Keep your back erect but not rigid.

Inhale through the nose, hold the breath for a few seconds; then exhale through the mouth. Repeat for 3 – 5 minutes. As you become more comfortable with this exercise, lengthen the seconds you hold your breath.

BUDDHA

EIGHTFOLD PATH OF BUDDHA

>   Even death is not to be feared by one
>   who has lived wisely

The man after whom Buddhism is named – Siddartha
Gautama – never ever claimed to be a God, a prophet, or a
supernatural being. In fact, when he was asked what he was,
Gautama simply said he was one who was "awake." In fact,
'Buddha' means 'awakened one.' Gautama was simply a
mortal man who was born and died but in between those two
events he taught the way to live with wisdom, compassion
and freedom from suffering. Though the body of literature
explaining and expounding Buddhism is extensive, the core
of all Buddhist teachings are based on Buddha's famous
eightfold path. These are the eight steps the Buddha taught
will put anyone on the path to enlightenment:

1. *Right understanding:* Accept life the way it is rather than cling
   to the way you wish it was. Understand that it is the clinging
   which causes you to suffer.

2. *Right thought.* Our thinking creates our reality so the Buddha
   stressed the importance of mind management. We can learn
   to think compassionately, kindly, with optimism and hope.
   We can remove from our minds anger, fear, guilt, anxiety and
   any other though which hold us down and back.

3. *Right speech.* This one's simple: don't lie, gossip, or speak
   harshly and negatively about other people. Rather, speak of
   them the way you would like to be spoken about by others.

4. *Right action.* Again this is pretty basic: no killing, no harming,
   no violence, and no substance abuse. Instead kindness,
   compassion, generosity and self-restraint.

5. Right livelihood (or right job). Those who wish to have their feet firmly planted on the path toward enlightenment should pursue work which is non-harming and non-violent. Here's how the Buddha himself said it: "Monks, a lay follower should not engage in five types of business. Which five? Business in weapons, business in human beings, business in meat, business in intoxicants, and business in poison. These are the five types of business that a lay follower should not engage in."

6. Right effort. This simply means doing the things you need to do to grow and evolve. Spiritual growth and evolution requires effort.

7. Right mindfulness. Pay attention. Don't live in the bubble of illusion. Be aware of who you are, what you do, and what's happening to you, in you and around you.

8. Right concentration. Meditate. It is meditation which leads to wisdom and skill in life. Do this regularly. Do this alone. Do this with a group. Do it both ways. Just do it!

BUDDHAS

DO YOU ACT LIKE FLY OR A BUDDHA

> Where there are humans,
> you'll find flies and Buddhas.
> **Kobayashi Issa**

The wandering poet and Buddhist teacher Kobayashi Issa was born in the little village of Kashiwabara in the mountains of Japan's Shinano Province on June 15, 1753 and died in the same village on January 5, 1828. In between those dates he learned the art of haiku and wandered the length and breadth of Japan, writing everywhere he went. Though his real name was Kobayashi Yataro, he chose Issa (Cup-of-Tea) as his haiku pen name. He often called himself "Shinano Province's Chief Beggar" and "Priest Cup-of-Tea of Haiku Temple." A devout Buddhist, the themes which he returned to repeatedly in his writings and teachings include: reincarnation, life's impermanence, compassion, and the joyful celebration of the ordinary. His quote cited above is worth further consideration: *where there are humans, you'll find flies and Buddhas.*

That wisdom is readily understood: we can be like the Buddha: compassionate and wise or we can be like flies which linger and hover over garbage. Issa is teaching that we should be kind not cruel. This is easily grasped. However, it is not so easily practiced. Consider this story about Zen students who came to their teacher, Master Bankei 1622-1693. They presented him with a petition signed by all the students in his school asking Bankei to expel one of the students. Evidently this student was a thief and had been caught stealing. All the others were outraged that this would happen in a Zen school and demanded his expulsion adding that if the thief did not leave, they would. Bankei call all the pupils together. He began the meeting by complimenting them on their high moral values and then added: "But our poor brother does not yet know right from wrong. Who will teach him if I do not? You all may leave if you wish; he stays." Bankei's wisdom was recognized immediately by his students. They reconsidered their own attitudes, remained in the school and harmony was again restored.

Where there are humans, you'll find flies and Buddhas. Like Bankei's students there are times we need to adjust our attitudes so they harmonize more with kindness and compassion rather than with judgment and condemnation. And, like Bankei we must take it upon ourselves to ensure that humans who are like flies are helped to discover their Buddha nature and hopefully become Buddhas.

C

CHANGE

CREATING PERSONAL CHANGE AND GROWTH

> There's only one corner of the universe you can
> be certain of improving, and that's your own self.
> **Aldous Huxley**

After many months of consideration and inner struggle, a
samurai in medieval Japan quit his position. This amounted
to desertion and according to the samurai code, was deeply
dishonorable. Of course, the man did not intend to be
dishonest but was simply responding to an inner voice calling
him to a vocation in the Zen life. He spent years at a
mountain monastery studying and meditating. Then he set off
on a pilgrimage. Before long he encountered a samurai on
horseback who recognized him and called him a dishonorable
being. The samurai reached for his sword intending to strike
the man down but decided the man was not worth dirtying his
sword over. Instead, he spat in the monk's face.

In the simple act of wiping away the spit, the monk realized
how far he traveled spiritually. In the past his reaction to such
an insult would have been swift and vicious. Deeply moved
by his inner composure and peace, he turned toward the
mountain where he had trained. As he approached the
monastery, he bowed and said: "The mountain is the
mountain, and the Way is the same as of old. Yet what has

changed is my own heart."

When an unpleasant person treats you in an unpleasant way how do you respond? Is your reaction different from the way you may have responded at an earlier time? Are you growing and maturing as a person emotionally and spiritually?

CLARITY

MIND CONTROL RESULTS IN CLARITY

> Tigers, lions, elephants, bears, snakes, all enemies, guardians of hells and demons become controlled by controlling the mind alone. By subduing the mind alone, you subdue them all.
> **Shantideva**

The Buddha was a traveling teacher moving from village to village. On one journey he passed by a lake. Thirsty, he asked one of his companions to bring him some water. The man walked to the lake just as several men in boats rowed by. As a result of the water became very muddy and murky so the man hesitated to draw water thinking to himself: "How can I give this muddy water to the Buddha to drink?" Returning he explained to the Buddha: "The water in there is very muddy. I don't think it is fit to drink."

An hour later, the Buddha asked the same man to go back to the lake. Still, the water was muddy and murky so he returned telling the Buddha. After some more time passed, the Buddha asked the man to go back to the lake and bring water. This time, the disciple found the sediment had settled.

The water was clean and clear. So he carefully collected water in several pots bringing it to the Buddha and his companions.

Looking into the water, the Buddha – never missing a teaching moment – said to the disciple: "See what you did to make the water clean and healthy. You simply let it be and the mud settled down on its own. Now you have clear water. This is much like your mind as well. When it is disturbed, just let it be. Give it a little time. It will settle down on its own. You don't have to put in any effort to calm it down. It will happen. It is effortless."

The Buddha was explaining the simplicity and the power of meditation. Meditation is easily accessible; anyone can do; and everyone benefits from it. Meditation is the tool for mind control. And when we meditate, the result is clarity and inner-peace because we allow the mental sediment to settle.

The great Indian Buddhist teacher Shantideva put it this way: *Tigers, lions, elephants, bears, snakes, all enemies, guardians of hells and demons become controlled by controlling the mind alone. By subduing the mind alone, you subdue them all.*

Here is a simple meditation to get you started. Find a quiet place where there will be no distractions. Sit comfortable in a chair or on the floor. Gently close your eyes and breathe deeply. Count your breaths – an inhalation and exhalation is one count. Count to five and then start over again at one. Do this for five minutes at a time. Practice this meditation technique several times a week, gradually expanding the time from five minutes to 15.

COMPASSION

LIVING YOUR LIFE OUT OF COMPASSION

> When a person responds to the joys and sorrows
> of others as though they were his own, he has
> attained the highest spiritual union."
> **Bhagavad Gita**

There is no authentic spiritual life without compassion for all beings. That is the teaching of these words from the Bhagavad Gita. This same teaching appears in the Christian New Testament: "Whoever does not love does not know God, because God is love." (1 John 4:8)

One of the most dramatic examples of someone whose life shows this teaching was American businessman Arthur Nash who found himself in an awkward business situation. A factory owner who rented space from Nash ran a sweatshop. As a landlord, Nash didn't know much about the man's business but when it started to fail and the man couldn't pay the rent, Nash took it over. When it came time to pay the employees, Nash was shocked to learn that some workers in the garment factory were paid as little as $4 per week, a very low amount even in 1918 when the incident took place. This upset Nash creating an ethical dilemma for him because his own business was struggling and his company had lost money the previous year. When Nash told his son he wanted to raise the sweatshop workers' wages, the son objected, reminding his father their own financial foundation was weakening daily.

Nevertheless, Nash decided that as long as the sweatshop operated he would pay fair wages so he called the employees together telling them: "I want you to know that brotherhood is a reality with me. You are all my brothers and sisters, children of the same great Father that I am, and entitled to all the justice and fair treatment that I want for myself. And so long as we run this shop....I am going to treat you as my brothers and sisters, and the Golden Rule is going to be our only governing law." Nash then told them he was tripling the wages of the lowest paid workers and doubling those of the highest paid. Not surprisingly, the business began to flourish.

CONFIDENCE

TEN AFFIRMATIONS FOR BUILDING CONFIDENCE

To change the subconscious pattern and increase its vibration, we must remold with new ideas and new concepts its magnetic forces. This can be done through the power of affirmation.
Satguru Sivaya Subramuniyaswami

Teachers from the East consistently remind people about the power of affirmations. Reciting short, positive statements remolds the putty-like substance which makes up the subconscious areas of the mind. We become what we affirm. Here are ten affirmations for building confidence:

1. I can! I will! I am able!

2. I am filled with creative energy and divine light.

3. I create my life anew each day.

4. I am guided as my life unfolds and evolves.

5. I am equal to whatever challenge I meet.

6. I am strong, energetic, and creative.

7. This is an abundant universe with plenty for all.

8. My inner wisdom guides me today.

9. I attract the best into my life.

10. I am a channel for the creative power of the universe.

Today, select one of these which intuitively appeals to you. Whenever you think of it during the day, recite it off and on all day long.

CONFUCIUS

WISDOM FROM CONFUCIUS

> To be wronged is nothing unless you
> continue to remember it.
> **Confucius**

Though Confucius (551-479 BCE) lived and taught more than 2400 years ago, his influence is still widely felt in China and around the world. Courses on Confucius and his wisdom continue to be added to university courses all over the world. This remarkable individual founded the first Chinese Wisdom School and his teachings continue to impact life in China, Japan and Korea.

As a youth, Confucius read widely and learned from many teachers. As his confidence grew, he began to teach gathering a group of pupils around him. His "career" was filled with successes and failures. Dismissed from his position, he was forced to become an itinerant traveling teacher, teaching where ever he could find students all the time hoping that his views on public life would take hold. By the time he died at the age of 72, he had become the dominant teacher of his era. Here is some wisdom from Confucius to reflect upon:

It does not matter how slowly you go, as long as you do not stop.

A man who has made a mistake and doesn't correct it is making another mistake.

Before you embark on a journey of revenge, dig two graves.

Forget injuries; never forget kindnesses.

By three methods we may learn wisdom. First by reflection which is noblest. Second by imitation, which is easiest. Third by experience, which is the bitterest.

The superior man blames himself; the inferior man blames

others.

It is easy to hate and difficult to love. This is how the whole scheme of things works. All good things are difficult to achieve; and bad things are very easy to achieve.

What you do not want done to yourself, do not do to others.

The superior man loves his soul; the inferior man loves his property. The superior man always remembers how he was punished for his mistakes; the inferior man always remembers the gift he receives.

To know what you know and know what you don't know is the characteristic of one who knows.

CONTEMPLATION

THOUGHT FOR FOOD

> In this food, I see clearly the presence
> of the entire universe supporting my existence.
> **Thich Nhat Hanh**

Many Buddhist communities practice "five contemplations" or thoughts before beginning to eat. Consider their approach.

1. *Gratitude*: They give thanks for the food, how it came to them. They reflect on the food's growth from seed to flowering plant. The people who work to get the food into a kitchen: those who harvest the plant, those who deliver it to

market, those who prepare it for sale, etc.

2. *Humility*: They are aware that many people on the planet don't have access to food, no matter what the price. There is also awareness that food affordability is dependent upon migrant laborers who pluck, pick and pull fruits and vegetables for very small payment.

3. *Restraint:* They avoid indulging their tastes and eating more than they need and more than is their rightful share. They eat everything on their plate so food is not wasted but are careful not to pile the plates with more than they can eat.

4. *Health:* They view, as does the Chinese tradition, that food is also medicine. So, the preparation is done in ways that are healthy and nutritious for the body not detrimental.

5. *Purpose:* Through the eating of food, they link the purpose of life with the eating of food. Eating is to nourish the body so that we can continue further progress on the path to enlightenment.

So, the next time you eat a meal, try do so with this same spirit of meditative mindfulness. Remember Thich Nhat Hanh's observation: *In this food, I see clearly the presence of the entire universe supporting my existence.*

D

DANA

REVERSE PANHANDLING

> Nobody made a greater mistake than
> he who did nothing because
> he could only do a little.
> **Edmund Burke**

Generosity is so important in Buddhism that there are many words for the various ways of being generous. (This is much like the Eskimo language which has many words for snow). One Buddhist word for generosity is *Dana* and it translates as "distribution of gifts". Could the following be an example?

Once a year a man in the Los Angeles area practices what he calls "reverse panhandling" He goes to the exit ramp of a major California freeway and, like other homeless people, holds up a cardboard sign. However, unlike the homeless whose signs read: "Will work for Food" or "Please Help", his signs read: "I need to give" or "I love to help" or "Please take my money." And, he is there with handfuls of $10 dollar bills giving them to any driver who extends his or her arm. Each time he's out there, he gives away approximately $1000.

Dana – the distribution of gifts.

I presented this story to a group recently asking what they thought of the man's actions. The responses varied:

"He's grandstanding" one individual said skeptically.

"He's changing a social paradigm from taking to giving" said another.

"He's obviously not attached to a thousand dollars," was another comment.

Still others said that his action made them re-think their own levels of generosity and how they could be generous to more people in more way on more occasions.

Whether his approach is one to model may be questionable. However, what's not questionable is the concept of *dana* – the distribution of our gifts. This is something all of need to do more of. A friend of mine was recently eating alone at a restaurant. In the booth next to him was a young mother with three boys. He overheard her explaining to the boys "this is a special time and this isn't something we can do often," she said. My friend realized this was a single mother on a tight budget treating her boys to a meal at a restaurant. He called over the manager giving him his credit card saying: "Please use my card to pay for everything this family order this evening. And, don't tell them who is paying." My friend then left the restaurant leaving his credit card behind. He returned a few hours later to pickup his card and the meal receipt. The manager sincerely thanked him and said: "When I told the mother that someone was paying for her meal, she began to weep out of amazement and delight."

That's a stellar example of *dana* – the distribution of our gifts.

DAY

BUDDHIST WAY FOR A WONDERFUL DAY

> Good morning life! I am so grateful
> to be alive today!
> **Modern Affirmation**

A sad number of people rise each day filled with negativity, dismay and frustration. It's exhibited as they rise and think to themselves....

Not another day!

I don't want to get up!

Only 3, 4, 5 ...days before it's the weekend.

I can't Mondays

I wish I didn't have to get up.

I hate my job.

I hate my life.

If any of those kinds of comments resonate with you, then consider this Buddhist way to greet each day which is much better because it sets a tone for joy and happiness. One example is this daily affirmation which residents of Thich Nhat Hanh's Plum Village community make upon rising from bed:

Waking up this morning, I smile.

24 brand new hours are before me.

I vow to live fully in each moment

and to look at all beings with eyes of compassion.

This short affirmation is worth memorizing and reciting every morning as your first thought for the day. It will get your day off to a positive start.

DELUSION

BEING ON GUARD AGAINST DELUSION

> The heart itself creates delusion.
> **Sosan** (Chinese Zen Master, died 606)

The Buddha told of a man who was widowed early in his marriage and left the single parent of a 9 year-old son who he loved very much. While away on a brief tip, bandits came to the man's village pillaging and destroying property. They took away several young men including the widower's son.

When the man returned he panicked at the sight of the ruins. Looking around he found a burnt corpse of a child and began to cry uncontrollably.

Convinced it was his beloved son, he organized a funeral ritual and cremation ceremony. He carefully collected the remains (ashes) placing them in a beautifully embroidered bag which he always kept at his side.

A few weeks later, his son escaped from the bandits and found his way home. He arrived at his father's hut after dark and knocked. The father, still in grief, asked: "Who is it?" The youth said, "It's me father. Open the door."

Unbelievably, the man refused to believe what he heard and wouldn't open the door telling the boy to "go away." After some time the child left. Father and son never saw each other again.

After telling this story, the Buddha made this point: "Sometime, somewhere, you take something be the truth. If you cling to it so much, even when the truth comes in person and knocks on your door, you will not open it."

Sometimes delusion is disguised as truth. That's why must be open and honest with ourselves always being on guard against delusion.

DEMONS

DEFEATING OUR DEMONS

> When we face our trials and troubles - however
> unwelcome they may be - with detachment and
> calmness, the way to proceed will present itself.
> **Victor M. Parachin**

Tibetans are fond of a story about their greatest spiritual
teacher, Milarepa (1052-1135 CE). As a young man he
developed a craving to know the Truth and as a result, the
mountains and caves began attracting him. Sitting in remove
caves high in the Himalayas he spent months in meditation.

Once he found himself in a cave inhabited by a great
company of demons all of whom distracted him from his
spiritual pursuit. First, he tried to subdue and suppress his
awareness of their presence. When that didn't work he
decided to honor them and extend compassion and friendship
toward them. Half of them left the cave. He then turned to the
remaining group welcoming them and inviting them to
observe him and accompany him. At that invitation, the
demons left his cave except for one particularly stubborn and
persistent demon. With no concern for his own safety,
Milarepa went to the demon placing his head in its mouth as
an offering. The demon disappeared without a trace and
never returned to bother Milarepa again.

Milarepa's experience can be our experience. Like him, all of
us face demons in the form of troubles, trials, traumas,
temptations. Consider doing what Milarepa did: rather than
fighting with them or trying to suppress them, welcome them
as guests in your life. When we learn to face our challenges,
however unwelcome they are - with calmness, compassion
and detachment the way to proceed will present itself.

DESIRES

ARE YOU TOO ATTACHED TO YOUR DESIRES?

> Overcoming attachment does not mean becoming cold
> and indifferent. On the contrary, it means learning to have
> relaxed control over our mind.
> **Kathleen McDonald**

Here's a story which many find hard to believe yet it's true. A
prominent yogi was invited to teach meditation workshops in
Texas. Arriving to register on the first day was a tall Texan,
complete with a large white cowboy hat, a visibly holstered
gun with a pearl handle on his side and two gorgeous women,
one on each arm. Seeing the yogi, the Texan approached him
saying: "I've come here because I'm really interested in
meditation but I want to know if, in doing this, I have to give
up guns, women and liquor. If the answer is 'yes' then I don't
want to participate," he said bluntly. The yogi responded
saying that he was there to just instruct meditation adding:
"I'm here to tell you or anyone else how to live or what you
have to give up." The Texan said he was fine with that,
registered (with his two girlfriends), and sat through the
entire four days of training.

Later, the yogi was invited back to the same city to offer the
meditation instruction again. The Texan showed up telling the
yogi: "You lied to me last year when you said I wouldn't have
to give up my guns, women and liquor." Puzzled, the yogi
said: "But I never told you to give up anything!" To which
the Texan replied: "Yes, but now that you taught me to
meditate I don't want those things anymore."

It's worth thinking a bit more about what happened to the

Texan. Of course, there's nothing wrong having a desires. It's when the desire becomes addictive and all consuming. There's nothing wrong with desiring a fine meal unless eating becomes gluttony. There's nothing wrong with desiring a glass of wine unless the desire becomes so strong that alcoholism results. Via meditation, the Texan learned to have what Kathleen McDonald calls "relaxed control" over his mind. The attachment to his desires was broken.

Meditation is an invaluable tool for freeing us from being overly attached to our desires. Meditation is a powerful method for shaping our lives in ways that are balanced and healthy.

DIFFICULTIES

WEATHERING HARD TIMES BETTER

> A wise man adapts himself to circumstances,
> as water shapes itself to the vessel
> that contains it.
> **Chinese Wisdom Saying**

Right mindfulness is number 7 on the Buddhist eightfold path. It refers to the mental discipline which will allow us to be open and accepting of the full range of life's experiences. Of course, it's easy to accept life's pleasant moment. More challenging is to be accepting, open, detached about life's pains and problems. Yet, that is exactly what right mindfulness is all about, learning to receive what is unpleasant and unwelcomed. One who explains and expounds this principle eloquently is the 13 century Islamic poet, Rumi. His poem is titled *Guest House:*

This being human is a guest house
Every morning a new arrival.
A joy, a depression, a meanness,
some momentary awareness comes
as an unexpected visitor.
Welcome and entertain them all!
Even if they are a crowd of sorrows,
who violently sweep your house
empty of its furniture,
still treat each guest honorably.
He may be clearing you out for some new delight.
The dark thought, the shame, the malice,
meet them at the door laughing,
and invite them in.
Be grateful for whoever comes,
because each has been sent
as a guide from beyond.

Following Rumi's counsel means letting go, relinquishing control and simply accepting life as it is. This is the most effective way of weathering a hard time in life.

DIGNITY

DEVELOPING A SACRED PRECEPTION

The saints are what they are, not because their
Sanctity makes them admirable to others,
but because the gift of sainthood makes it possible for
them to admire everybody else.
Thomas Merton

Think what a beautiful place this world would be if all of us treated others with respect and reverence. Consider how much gentler the planet would be if we acknowledged the dignity and divinity of everyone we encountered. The Dalai Lama is one who views others through this sacred perception. While giving a series of lectures in San Francisco, the Dalai Lama was provided a room in a hotel where prominent and even famous individuals stayed. Just before departing, he informed the hotel management he would like to thank, in person, the staff who made his stay so comfortable. The Dalai Lama extended an invitation for any hotel employees who wished to meet him. On his last morning at the hotel a long line of housekeepers, cooks, servers, custodians, receptionists, managers and maintenance workers stood along the circular driveway at the hotel entrance. The Dalai Lama slowly walked down the line greeting, touching, and speaking with each person.

Perhaps you can look back over your life and recall a moment when someone treated you with dignity, respect, graciousness, trust and love. Is it not possible for you to do the same for others. Perhaps you could try this today: *Rather than focus on a person's faults and flaws, remind yourself it never hurts to think too highly of any person.* Viewing everyone you encounter with a sacred perception will ennoble them and empower them to act better and be better because of your perception.

DIRECTION

WE MOVE IN THE DIRECTION OF OUR THOUGHTS

It is the nature of thought to find its way into action.
Christian Nevell Bovee

A father wanting to teach his son how to ride a bike, took the boy to the large parking lot at a nearby school. Since it was a weekend, the lot was entirely empty. The only object was a bike stand on one side. The dad helped his son mount the bike, gave it a gentle push and the boy was pleasantly surprised at his ability to control the bike. As he rode, however, he saw the bike stand and began saying to himself: "A bike stand! I can't hit the bike stand!" knowing it caused him to crash and fall off the bike.

As he rode, the bike came closer and closer to the bike stand. "Just don't hit the bike stand," he kept saying to himself.

Of course, on that empty parking lot he drove right into the bike stand, crashed and fell off his bike. Fortunately, he had only minor scratches and bruises. That experience – and it's a common one for children first learning to ride a bike – offers this Buddhist lesson about the mind: *we move in the direction of our thoughts.*

The boy's bike ride could have had an entirely different outcome if he simply thought about the wide open space available to him. Instead, he focused on the bike stand and rode right into it. As adults, we're not much different from that boy in terms of thoughts. Too often we focus and think about the problem rather than the solutions which are available. Though opportunities abound, we seem to get entrapped with a focus on the obstacle in the way. Or consider emotional thoughts. A person who has angry thoughts will likely result an angry outburst. On the other hand, a person who has thoughts of compassion will likely result in kind acts.

So, every time you find yourself thinking in a negative, pessimistic way, pause to re-direct your thoughts into a hopeful, positive ways. Remember, we move in the direction of our thoughts!

DIVINITY

YOU ARE DIVINE!

> You are here to realize your inner divinity and manifest your innate enlightenment.
> **Morihei Ueshiba**

With those few words, Morihei Ueshiba (1883-1969), founder of the Japanese martial art of aikido answers a philosophical-spiritual question many people have: "What is the purpose of my life?" His response: *You are here to realize your inner divinity and manifest your innate enlightenment.* Though he's correct, tapping into our inner divinity and acting upon our innate enlightenment is difficult because we have expended great effort to cover up our divinity. We often do this because of life's threats and cruelties. Rather than remain open, available and therefore vulnerable, we protect ourselves from potential harm and injury. There is an interesting historical analogy to this psychological defense mechanism.

Inside a large temple north of Thailand's ancient capital, Sukotai, there once stood an enormous and ancient clay Buddha. Though not considered a particularly refined work of Thai Buddhist art, the clay Buddha was carefully cared for over a five hundred year period. Gradually it came to be revered and honored for its survival and longevity. During those five hundreds, the Buddha endured violent storms, invading armies and changes of government. It was the one constant in an otherwise changing environment.

Then, the monks who looked after the temple noticed the statue had begun to crack. As the weather became hotter and drier, the crack became so wide that a curious monk took his flashlight to peer inside. He was stunned to see that behind the clay, was glittering gold. Chipping and scraping away the outside clay, temple residents discovered one of the largest gold images of Buddha ever created in Southeast Asia. Today, the uncovered Golden Buddha draws crowds of pilgrims and tourists from all over Thailand and around the world. The monks assume the Golden Buddha was covered in plaster and clay to protect it during times of conflict and unrest.

There is something of us in that story. We are born with divinity inside but threatening situations of all kinds - emotional, spiritual, intellectual, physical - have prompted us to cover up our innate divine nature. Each one of us needs to look carefully at ourselves and see that beneath the clay and plaster is original goodness, compassion, divinity. In the east this is called our Buddha nature. Even Judaism and Christianity offer a similar thought. The book of Genesis notes: "God created man in his own image--in the mage of God he created him; male and female." (Genesis 1:27) Jesus taught: "the kingdom of God is within you." (Luke 17:21). And, twice in his writings, St. Paul speaks of our inner divinity. In 1 Corinthians 6:19 he said: "Your body is a temple of the Holy Spirit, who is in you, whom you have received from God." In another writing, he reminded early followers of the "Christ in you." (Colossians 1:27)

Every time you look into a mirror, try reminding yourself that you are looking at a Buddha, at a Christ. See and sense your inner nobility, dignity, beauty, and divinity. Rather than live out of a limited, fearful, impoverished identity, live as a person who is on an enlightened path. Be a blessing in your part of the world.

E

ELASTICITY

PRACTICING ELASTICITY

> The wise are always flexible, pliable, resilient and elastic.
> The less wise remain rigid, firm stiff and unyielding.
> **Victor M. Parachin**

The Buddha told this story of man walking along a road and arriving at a great river. It is wide, rapidly flowing and dangerous. The man knows he must cross over to the other side in order to continue his journey. He begins to collect wood and foliage for binding twine in order to make a raft. When it's complete, he paddles across the river, and reaches the other shore safely.

Now suppose that, after he reaches the other shore, he takes the raft and puts it on his head and walks with it on his head wherever he goes. "Would he be using the raft in an appropriate way?" the Buddha asks. "No, a reasonable man will realize that the raft has been very useful to him in crossing the river and arriving safely on the other shore, but that once he has arrived, it is proper to leave the raft behind and walk on without it."

This is using the raft appropriately the Buddha explained adding: "In the same way, all truths should be used to cross over; they should not be held on to once you have arrived. You should let go of even the most profound insight or the most wholesome teaching; all the more so, unwholesome teachings."

Via that story the Buddha is teaching that we need to practice spiritual, mental and emotional elasticity. Rather than holding onto views and attitudes which no longer serve us, we must acknowledge their past usefulness and then release them. The wise among us will always be flexible, pliable resilient and elastic not rigid, firm, stiff and unyielding.

EMERSON

GURU EMERSON

> In all nations there are minds which incline to dwell in the conception of fundamental unity. This tendency finds its highest expression in the religious writings of the east, chiefly in the Indian scriptures.
> **Ralph Waldo Emerson**

One of the first Americans to study Vedic thought as found in Hinduism and Buddhism was the Unitarian minister Ralph Waldo Emerson. Easily departing from his Christian orientation, Emerson became intrigued with Eastern spirituality finding much in it which resonated with his spirit. Here are some of his comments about eastern philosophy which became part of his world view:

On inner-divinity:
Be true to yourself; because every person has within him/her something really divine.

On the law of karma:
Cause and effect, means and ends, seed and fruit, cannot be severed, for the effect already blooms in the cause, the end pre-exists in the means, the fruit in the seed.

You cannot do wrong without suffering wrong.
On reincarnation:
The secret of the world (is) that all things subsist, and do not die, but only retire a little from slight and afterwards return again.

Through all of his writings and lectures, more and more eastern philosophy came to expressed so much so that sages in India came to admire him. In an essay entitled *Emerson as Seen from India*, written shortly after his death, Pratap Hunder Mozoomdar, an Indian teacher noted: "Emerson... shines upon India serene as the evening star. He seems to some of us to have been a geographical mistake."

EMOTIONS

SKILLFULLY MANAGING SADNESS AND GLADNESS

> He who would be serene and pure needs
> but one thing, detachment.
> **Meister Eckhart**

Here's an ancient eastern story known even by many in the West. It comes from the ancient *Huainanzi* text, a Chinese classic dating back to the 2nd century BCE which blends Taoist and Confucianist philosophies. This story is so favored and well known among the Chinese that they have summarized it in a two sentence proverb: *Sai ong loses horse. Who knows if it isn't a Blessing.*

On the northern frontier of ancient China lived a man who was skilled in raising horses. He was very well known and referred to by most as *Sai Ong* - literally, "Old Frontiersman."

One day his prized horse escaped and ran off into the Hu territory beyond the Great Wall. At the time the Hu tribes were hostile toward the Chinese, so the assumption was his horse was gone for good. This loss was significant, much like someone today having their brand new, uninsured, luxury vehicle stolen. Lamenting his great financial setback, many visited Sai Ong to express sympathy. However, Sai Ong's elderly father, who was at his son's side, surprised the visitors because he seemed so calm and unaffected. To their amazement, the older man asked: "Who says this cannot be some sort of blessing?"

Several months later, the prized stallion returned to the stable bringing with him a fine steed. Suddenly Sai Ong's wealth doubled. People came by marvel at the turn of events and to offer hearty congratulations. Again, the elderly father was restrained saying: "Who says this cannot be some kind of misfortune?" Sai Ong enjoyed training and riding horses so he took the new horse out for a ride. An accident occurred causing him to fall off the animal breaking his leg. Sympathetic people came to console the family and again they experienced an elderly serene and calm simply telling them: "Who says this cannot be some sort of blessing?"

Sometime later, the Hu army crossed the border into China.

All able-bodied young men were conscripted into military service to defend the nation. A series of fierce battles ensued resulting in heavy casualties. Among those recruited from the northern frontier, nine out of ten men were killed in battle. One of the few young men spared was Sai Ong's son. Because of his broken leg, he was not pressed into military service and, thus, his family survived that period of war intact.

Though this story is familiar to Westerners, its interpretation and understanding needs some clarification. The story is about better management of sadness and gladness. *It warns against the danger of turning trauma into drama.* When we experience misfortune and tragedy, we become despondent. When we experience something greatly advantageous, we become ecstatic. The problem with these two extremes is that life is lived on an emotional roller coaster. The phrase *Sai ong loses horse. Who knows if it isn't a Blessing?* speaks directly to life's harsh and painful events. The proverb is a reminder that things my not need to be as they initially appear.

What is often forgotten, however, is that the same phrase ought to be applied when something advantageous comes our way. Just as every cloud has a silver lining, every silver lining contains a dark cloud. Of course, it does not mean we shouldn't feel sadness or gladness. We are not emotionless robots wandering the planet. It does remind us that the path of moderation is a more skillful response to life's ups and downs. *Sai ong loses horse. Who knows if it isn't a blessing?* Our culture has a similar proverbial warning: *Be careful what you wish for!*

ENDINGS

CREATING A NEW ENDING

> Start with what you know.
> Mature according to nature.
> Let destiny do the rest.
> **Chuang Tzu**

Sometimes it's not possible to go back and make a new start. It is, however, always possible to start from now and create a brand new ending. Here's a highly inspiring example of a man who did just that. Because of substance abuse, he found himself out of a job, a marriage and without the trust of his children. It finally dawned on him that he needed to change his life.

Uncertain how to do that or what step to take next, he wandered into a used book store spending hours on the floor surrounded by spiritual and self-help books. Finally, he bought the only book he could afford – it was $1.20 and he had $1.50. The book a technical manual of Zen training. It contained detailed chapters such as: "How Junior Priests Must Behave in the Presence of Senior Priests"; "Mealtime Regulations"; "Triainees Hall Rules"; and "Instructions To The Chief Cook." The book would not be one most people would be remotely interested in. Yet, he was enthralled reading through the book in one sitting. What struck him was the beauty he saw in the monastic discipline, attention to detail and self-control. Those were all things he felt were lacking in his own life.

Upon turning the last page, he discovered that the previous owner had placed a sticker there with his name and address on it. The homeless man used the last of his money to buy a stamp and wrote the man telling him how much he enjoyed the book. Within days, he received a letter back from the original book owner who invited him to attend a meditation group in the community. So, the homeless man began attending but the book owner was never there. To this day he has never met the man who owned the book.

However, he became a regular meditation attendee spending a year attending lectures, meditating on his own and reading books about Buddhism. As he grew and deepened spiritually, he felt compelled to share his insights with other homeless people so he began holding meditation sessions under a bridge where many homeless in his area congregated. That must surely be the most unusual meditation group in the country. Little by little, homeless men and women began to join him to sit in meditation often leaving him gifts of used clothing, bits of food and small amounts of money.

Today, that formerly homeless man is an advocate for the homeless in his community and continues working to bring them spiritual and physical services. He is a powerfully inspiring example of the truth that though there are times when we can't go back and make a new start, we can start from now and create a brand new ending for our lives.

ENERGIES

WHAT HAPPENS WHEN YOU'RE AROUND?

> The entire ocean is affected by a pebble.
> **Blaise Pascal**

Sera Je is one of Tibet's oldest and largest monastic universities. It was founded in 1491, educating and training thousands of monks. Until the Chinese invaded Tibet in 1959, Sera Je was one of the most prestigious and important centers of Tibetan Buddhism. The story is told of one great Tibetan master who was a highly regarded scholar and abbot of Sera Je. At one time, this master adopted a cat who lived with him. From the time he brought the cat into his life and into the monastery, everyone noticed immediately that the cat stopped catching and eating mice. This was unusual for at least two reasons. First, it is in the nature of every cat to chase, capture and eat mice. Secondly, because Buddhists take seriously *ahimsa* or non harming, they refuse to kill mice which results in monasteries often becoming safe breeding grounds for these creatures.

The conclusion which observers of the cat came to was this: the cat was permanently changed and deeply influenced by its association with the abbot who had a tamed mind, a peaceful spirit, and a pure heart. Even when the cat saw mice running around the room, it would remain quietly, peacefully by the abbot's side.

That simple account is a reminder that the energies we expend affect everything around us (including our domestic companions). It raises this profound question: what's happening when you're around? What kind of energy are you sending out? When you're around, do things become peaceful, quiet and gentle or frenzied, chaotic, confusing? Reflect on Blaise Pascal's sentence: *The entire ocean is affected by a pebble.*

ENCOURAGEMENT

THE POWER OF ENCOURAGEMENT

> Be someone's cheerleader in life.
> **Victor M. Parachin**

One of the most fascinating exhibits in the Library of Congress is a display of the personal effects found on Abraham Lincoln the night he was shot. Those include a small handkerchief embroidered with A. Lincoln, a country boy's pocketknife, a spectacle case repaired with cotton string, a Confederate $5 bill and a nearly worn-out newspaper clipping praising his accomplishments as president. The newspaper story begins with this sentence: "Abe Lincoln is one of the greatest statesmen of all time."

Clearly, that clipping was an important source of affirmation for President Lincoln. Although today he is regarded as one of the nation's finest presidents, in his day he was extremely controversial and unpopular in some circles. The nation was bitterly divided. Major newspapers of the day blamed him and his leadership for the civil war. His life was constantly threatened. Thus, Lincoln needed something in his pocket to remind him that his critics were not his only observers. So he carried that newspaper clipping which reminded him that someone believed in him.

That vignette is an important reminder of the uplifting power of encouragement. This principle comes under numbers 3 and 4 of the Buddha's famous eightfold path. Number 3 is right speech and number 4 is right action.

Both of those involve the discipline of self-restraint from words and acts which are harsh, negative and unkind. Right speech and right action call for a generosity of spirit whereby we meet and greet everyone gently, kindly and affirmatively.

All people need to be touched by the uplifting power of encouragement. And this is a power which is within us. All we need to do is unleash the power of encouragement. Sometimes the difference between giving up and going on is encouragement - a simple hello; a quiet expression of concern; a few words of support; a compliment sincerely uttered. To be an encourager is something anyone can do and everyone benefits from.

ENLIGHTENMENT

WHAT IS ENLIGHTENMENT?

> Strictly speaking, there are no enlightened people.
> There is only enlightened activity.
> **Shunryu Suzuki**

There is an odd and unusual practice among some Zen communities. After a student has studied a lengthy period of time with a Zen master, he may ask for a certificate of enlightenment. If the Zen master concurs the student is enlightened, the certificate is given. Of course, this is both odd and foolish. Yet, it raises the questions "What is enlightenment?" and "Who is enlightened?" If you were to give someone a certificate of enlightenment, what are the qualities of the person who would receive it?

Here are some clues from Buddhism. First, the Buddha did not use the word "enlightened" in referring to himself. The term he used was a Sanskrit one, *bodhi,* which means *awakened.* Enlightened was a description ascribed to him later by others. Secondly, the Buddha taught that we humans suffer from three "poisons."

1. Greed.

2. Anger.

3. Ignorance.

He also taught that neither Buddhism nor meditation necessarily eradicate those three. What spiritual practice can do, however, is a) help us recognize the poisons when they appear in our lives and b) work to transform them. Thus,

1. Greed can turn into generosity.

2. Anger can be turned into compassion.

3. Ignorance can be turned into wisdom.

With this understanding, we can appreciate Shunryu Suzuki's observation that: *Strictly speaking, there are no enlightened people, there is only enlightened activity.* Enlightenment is a continual process not a definitive goal.

ENLIGHTENMENT – PART 2

NO SHORTCUTS TO ENLIGHTENMENT

All beings are from the very beginning Buddhas.
It is like water and ice: Apart from water, no ice,
outside living beings, no Buddhas. Not knowing it
is near they seek it afar, what a pity!
Osho

The Zen master Hakuin (1685-1768) often told his students about an old woman who owned a tea shop in the village. He explained she was exceptionally skilled in the tea ceremony adding that her understanding of Zen was deep and profound.

Many students were intrigued by his enthusiastic endorsement of the old woman so they would visit her tea shop hem-selves to check her out. Intuitively, whenever the old woman encountered the students she could tell immediately whether they had come to experience the tea or to probe her grasp of Zen. Those desiring tea were served graciously. For others who wanted to quiz her about Zen, she would hide until they approached her door and then would attack them with a fire poker. Only one out of ten such students managed to escape her beating.

A question to ask: why did she respond this way to the two types of students? The ones to want to quiz her about Zen were using her. They looked to her not for who she was but to get what they could out of her. She didn't like being used that way. What she was trying to convey to the students was that she didn't like being used for her knowledge of Zen. Persons have to find enlightenment on their own, in their own time, and way. There are no shortcuts to enlightenment.

Here's another question: If you approached that woman, would she serve you tea or attack you with the fire poker?

F

FAMILIAR

WHAT'S YOUR MIND FAMILIAR WITH?

> If you place your mind on thoughts that are
> based upon compassion and wisdom that's
> what the mind will become familiar with.
> **Sakyong Mipham Rinpoche**

The above quote is provocative because it raises this vital
question: *what's my mind 'familiar' with?* Or, if you'd like to
begin with our culture, ask the question differently: *what's
familiar to the mind of people in our society?*

The answer is as quick as it is obvious: violence, anger,
greed, frustration even rage. They are so 'familiar' to the mind
that they are easily, quickly and readily triggered by the
smallest of issues. What is _not_ familiar to the mind of people
in our culture are wisdom, compassion, kindness, civility etc.

That we become what we think was first taught by the
Buddha who succinctly said: "All that we are is the result of
what we have thought. The mind is everything. What we
think we become."

Building on this ancient Buddhist teaching are the words of

the contemporary Buddhist Sakyong Mipham - "If you place your mind on thoughts that are based upon compassion and wisdom that's what the mind will become familiar with."

This concept of feeding the mind with virtues versus vices appears in Native American teaching. The story is told of an Elder spending time with his young grandson. The Elder explains to his grandson that in all of his life, there have been two wolves battling inside of him. One wolf is prone to anger, hostility, and rage while the other is committed to kindness, compassion and wisdom. "Which one will win?" asks the grandson. "The one which I feed," says the Elder.

Interestingly, this Buddhist concept appears in the Christian bible as well where St. Paul writes: "you'll do best by filling your minds and meditating on things true, noble, reputable, authentic, compelling, gracious—the best, not the worst; the beautiful, not the ugly; things to praise, not things to curse." (Philippians 4:8-9, The Message Bible)

So, today do an emotional and spiritual inventory of yourself asking: *what's my mind familiar with?*

FEAR

BREAKING FEAR'S GRIP ON LIFE

> The wise man in the storm prays to God,
> not from safety from danger, but for
> deliverance from fear. It is the storm within
> that endangers him, not the storm without.
> **Ralph Waldo Emerson**

A man, after receiving a diagnosis of cancer, returned home in shock and in fear. Along with traditional treatment for cancer, he also began to meditate and found himself saying to the Universe: "I want to live. I want to live. I want to live."

Then he 'heard' a voice answer him saying: "You _are_ alive!"

And in that moment, the death grip of fear was released from him and he began to live more hopefully, optimistically and confidently. From time to time, it can be useful for us to remind ourselves: "I _am_ alive!"

That means, no matter what challenges and discouragements we face, we can make decisions, we can make changes, we can adapt and adjust, all the time moving our lives into desirable directions. Reminding ourselves: "I _am_ alive!" can break the stranglehold which fear has on our life. It's another way of doing what Emerson advises, asking the divine "not from safety from danger, but for deliverance from fear," because "it is the storm within that endangers him, not the storm without." Add to that, Franklin Roosevelt's wisdom: "The only thing we have to fear is fear itself."

FORGIVENESS

THE POWER OF FORGIVENESS

> Hatred does not cease by hatred, but only by love;
> this is the eternal rule.
> **Buddha**

A woman had a son who was beaten to death in a street fight.

His assailant was arrested, tried and sentenced to a long prison term. The mother asked to meet with him after his sentencing so that she could experience "closure" by telling him, face to face, how much she hated him for destroying her life. When she was ushered into the holding room to meet the assailant, she was stunned to see a boy standing in a corner, shackled and crying. He was hardly the horrendous, calloused criminal her mind had created.

"As I watched that boy, so forlorn - no parents, no friends, and no support - all I saw was another mother's son," she said. She began to cry, not for her son but for another mother's son and without thinking, she heard herself asking the boy: "Can I give you a hug?" As she felt his body against hers, she says her anger literally melted away replaced by a natural feeling of compassion and connection with this suffering human being.

This mother's act of forgiveness was an all too rare opening of the soul. Yet, her act is one which needs to be replicated by more of us. Her dramatic encounter in a prison holding room supports this truth: *forgiveness has the power to transform both the offended and the offender.* Whenever we hold resentment toward someone who has wounded us, we remain permanently attached to the pain inflicted. Forgiveness is the only way to dissolve that link and experience freedom from hurt. Forgiveness is an act of love toward ourselves and toward our offender. The Buddha was right when he said: "Hatred does not cease by hatred, but only by love."

FRIENDS

WATCH THE COMPANY YOU KEEP

> As water changes according to the soil through
> which it flows, so a person assimilates
> the character of his or her associates.
> **Tirukural** (Chapter 46)

Consider this wisdom from a Hindu ethical scripture called *Tirukural* "As water changes according to the soil through which it flows, so a person assimilates the character of his or her associates."

That ancient wisdom teaches that our state of consciousness and attitudes toward life are strongly influenced by the company we keep. Simply stated if we are surrounded by negative, cynical, pessimists then there is a good chance we will look out at life the same way. On the other hand, if we surround ourselves with positive, hopeful, optimists then it is highly likely we will look out at life that way.

Thus, the words from *Tirukural* instruct us to surround ourselves with people who are on a spiritual path seeking growth, evolution and higher consciousness. An ideal place to find people like that is in a yoga class, a meditation group, a faith community. The words in the *Tirukural* are a reminder that we absolutely _must_ choose the company we keep very, very carefully. We become like the people we meet and interact with.

G

GAPS

REDUCING THE GAP BETWEEN THE SACRED AND THE SECULAR

> Master Tun Kwo asked Chuang:
> "Show me where the Tao is to be found."
> Chuang Tzu replied:
> "There is nowhere it is not to be found."
> **The Way of Chuang Tzu**

Have you ever felt that you were too busy, too tired, too preoccupied, too pressured by life to devote much time to spiritual practice? If so, you will find this encounter between the Buddha and an elderly grandmother enlightening.

This woman was courageous enough to approach Buddha and ask: "Master, I want very much to live a spiritual life but I am now too old and too feeble to withstand the rigor of monastic life. Also, I am too consumed with household duties to set aside periods of time for meditation. What can I do?"

Read carefully the Buddha's succinct reply:

"Every time you draw water from the well for you and your family, remain aware of every single act, movement, and motion of your hands. As you are carrying home the water jug atop your head, be aware of every step of your feet. As you do your chores, maintain continuous mindfulness and awareness every single instant, moment after moment, and you too will become a master of meditation."

The Buddha's encounter is a reminder that when we live more mindfully we will become aware that opportunities for our spiritual growth and evolution are ever present. It doesn't matter if the bulk of our time is spent in a corporate boardroom, hospital, school, home, clinic, retail store or even in prison, life provides ample opportunities to develop and deepen spiritual practices. Chuang Tzu, who is believed to lived in China in the Fourth or Third Century BCE and who enlarges on the teachings of Lao Tzu, answers correctly when he is asked: "Show me where the Tao (the spiritual path) is to be found." His answer; "There is nowhere it is not to be found." Perhaps today you could try to dissolve the distance between the sacred and the secular in your place of work. Here is a simple meditation you could quietly offer during the course of your work day wherever that may be. As you inhale say to yourself: *My work today . . .*

As you exhale say to yourself: *May it serve a greater good.*

GIANTS

JESUS & BUDDHA: SPIRITUAL GIANTS

> Jesus and the Buddha were teachers of a world-subverting wisdom that undermined and challenged conventional ways of seeing and being in their time and in every time.

During the Vietnam War, *Jack* Kornfield a Buddhist teacher, tells of visiting a temple built by a famous master simply known as the Coconut Monk. The temple was located on an island in the fertile Mekong Delta. Upon arrival the monks showed Kornfield around the temple and then took him to one end of the island. There, on the top of a hill, Kornfield saw an enormous 60 foot tall statue of a standing Buddha. Right beside him was an equally tall standing Jesus. They had their arms around each other and were smiling.

It was an impressive and hope-producing sight. As American helicopter gunships flew by and as the war raged around Buddha and Jesus, the two stood there like brothers. Those two towering figures were put side by side to emphasize the similarities between the teachings of Buddha and Jesus – and there are many. Consider these:

Buddha: *Hatred does not cease by hatred, but only by love; this is the eternal rule.*

Jesus: *Here's another old saying that deserves a second look: 'Eye for eye, tooth for tooth.' Is that going to get us anywhere? Here's what I propose: 'Don't hit back at all.' Live generously.*

Buddha: *The great cloud rains down on all whether their nature is superior or inferior. The light of the sun and the moon illuminates the whole world, both he, who does well and he, who does ill, both he, who stands high and he, who stands low.*

Jesus: *Your father in heaven makes his sun rise on the evil and on the good, and sends rain on the righteous and on the unrighteous.*

Buddha: *With the relinquishing of all thought and egotism, the enlightened one is liberated through not clinging.*

Jesus: *Those who want to save their life will lose it, and those who lose their life for my sake will save it.*

Jesus and the Buddha, two towering figures symbolized by the statues in the Mekong Delta – both try to point people in the direction of enlightenment.

{Note: To people whose past experiences with Christian churches have been hurtful or disappointing, it's worth remembering this distinction: *you can believe in the religion of Jesus but not the religion about Jesus.*)

GITA

SPIRITUAL GEMS FROM THE BHAGAVAD GITA

> In the morning I bathe my intellect in the stupendous and cosmogonal philosophy of the Bhagavad-gita, in comparison with which our modern world and its literature seem puny and trivial
> **Henry David Thoreau**

People who are interested in Eastern spirituality will, sooner or later, come across a quotation from the Bhagavad Gita.

Commonly referred to a simply "The Gita" it is universally renowned as the jewel of India's spiritual wisdom. Its 700 concise verses provide a definitive guide to the science of self-realization. The Gita is one of Hinduism's most popular and sacred scriptures. Bhagavad Gita (400-300 BCE) literally means "Lord's Song". It is a book of spiritual philosophy which records the conversation between the God Krishna and the warrior Prince Arjuna. At the time, Arjuna is about to engage in war. This "war" is a symbol of the conflicts, tensions and battles we all face in our daily lives. Krishna, responding to Arjuna's ambivalence, confusion and moral dilemma, explains to Arjuna his duties as a warrior and prince. With remarkable clarity, Krishna outlines to Arjuna the principles of right living. Krishna explains how people should conduct themselves on a day to day basis, keeping the Divine at the center of their awareness, and performing their duties without being attached to the outcomes. As a result, the Gita is described as a concise guide to Hindu philosophy and also as a practical guide for daily living. Here are some spiritual gems from the Bhagavad Gita:

Be compassionate. Not just to your friends but to everyone.

One can become whatever one wants to be, if one constantly contemplates on the object of desire with faith.

The power of God is with you at all times; through the activities of mind, sense, breathing and emotions; and is constantly doing all the work using you as a mere instrument.

Delusion arises from anger. the mind is bewildered by delusion. Reasoning is destroyed when the mind is bewildered. One falls down when reasoning is destroyed.

A man's own self is his friend; a man's own self is his foe.

I (God) am easily attained by the person who always remembers me and is attached to nothing else.

Another who was impacted by the Gita was Ralph Waldo Emerson who said: "I owed a magnificent day to the Bhagavad Gita. It was the first of books; it was as if an empire spoke to us, nothing small or unworthy, but large, serene, consistent, the voice of an old intelligence which in another age and climate had pondered and thus disposed of the same questions which exercise us."

GIVING

BEING BETTER GIVERS

> Think of giving not as a duty but as a privilege.
> **John D. Rockefeller**

Seicho Seisetsu (1274-1339) was the head monk and Zen master of the largest temple in Edo (the ancient name for Tokyo), Japan. Highly respected for his insights and lessons, the temple was filled and overcrowded week after week. Umeza Seibei, a prosperous merchant in the city decided to donate five hundred pieces of gold, called ryo, toward the construction of a larger facility. He brought the sack of gold coins to the teacher who said: "All right, I will take it."

Umeza gave him the sack of gold but was disappointed and dissatisfied with the Seisetsu's response. "A family could live an entire year on three ryo and I haven't even been thanked for five hundred," he thought to himself. Hinting for a warmer response, Umeza said: "In that sack are five hundred ryo."

"You told me that before," responded Seisetsu.

"Even if I am a wealthy man, five hundred ryo is a lot of money" Umeza reminded the master.

"Do you want me to thank you for it?" asked Seisetsu.

"You ought to," replied Umeza.

"Why should I?" inquired Seisetsu. "The giver should be thankful!"

The Zen master was obviously a no-nonsense kind of teacher. Unintimidated and unimpressed by Umeza's wealth, he spotted an opportunity to teach the wealthy merchant an important lesson about being a better giver. Often, patrons of art and culture give and expect something in return. For example, their names are placed on buildings in recognition of their gift. In such cases, it is not unfair to wonder if they are truly giving or merely buying naming rights.

However, let's not simply focus and pick on the wealthy but let's look at our own giving patterns. When we give anything - kindness, love, money - is it given without expectation of something in return? Or, are there strings attached? Seietsu's lesson is worthy of further reflection. The very fact that we are in a position to extend kindness, love and generosity ought to prompt us to be thankful that we can do so. Nothing else should be expected. *In fact, the one who gives ought to feel exactly the same joy and pleasure as the who is receiving.* And experiencing that pleasure and joy should be sufficient in itself. That may have been in the mind of philanthropist John D. Rockefeller when he said: "Think of giving not as a duty but as a privilege."

GIVE

GIVE AND YOU WILL RECEIVE!

> Wise people take the needs of all the people
> as their own. They are good to the good.
> But they are also good to those who are
> still absorbed in their own need.
> **Lao Tzu**

An honorable Japanese Samurai died in battle arriving at the heavenly doors. Upon being informed he would be entering the heavenly section of the life beyond, he asked if he could first see the hell section of the life beyond. So he was escorted to that partition and was surprised when he was led into a magnificent room. In it there were tables heaped with an abundance of the most desirable, delicious foods one could prepare. However, the people in the room were cursing and screaming in anger. Puzzled initially, the Samurai soon saw the problem. Everyone in that room had three foot long chopsticks tied to their arms. They had learned how to pick up the food with those chopsticks but, because they were so long, they were unable to place the food in their mouths. Consequently they were slowly starving in the very presence of abundant food.

When the Samurai was escorted into the heavenly partition he saw a similar scene. The room was filled with the same desirable, delicious food. Those present also had three foot long chopsticks tied to their arms. But, this room was not filled with frustration, anger and despair. Rather it was filled with sounds of laughter and joy. The difference: those in the heavenly partition learned to feed one another. In giving they received.

GOD

BE CAREFUL HOW YOU THINK ABOUT GOD

> All gods are one. There is no difference between a Hindu and a Muslim. Mosque and temple are the same.
> **Sri Sathya Sai Baba**

A man felt he was drifting aimlessly through life and was in need of spiritual guidance. So, he sought out a spiritual teacher. That teacher spent most of his time alone in meditation and study. He saw people infrequently and the wait to meet with him was long. After many months, the teacher agreed to an audience with the seeker. Keeping the conversation to a minimum, the teacher explained that the man is allowed to ask only one question. Thinking carefully, the seeker asks: "What is God really like?"

The master responded: "God? God is a carrot." Then the master laughed heartily.

Frustrated after the long wait and the seemingly ridiculous answer, the seeker felt mocked and insulted. He left greatly irritated by this spiritual teacher. After thinking about the encounter, the seeker's heart softened and he suspected that he may have misunderstood the teacher. So, he requested a second interview which does not take place for many months. Finally, he is summoned and the rule is the same: he can only ask one question.

This time the seeker is more prepared and seeks clarification: "What did you mean when you aid God is a carrot?" The teacher looked at the seeker in amazement saying: "A carrot? God is not a carrot! God is a radish!" Again, the teacher laughs heartily over his comment.

Once again, the seeker left feeling frustrated, irritated, and convinced the teacher is a fraud, simply playing with seekers. He broods and reflects on those two encounters for a long time. Then, one day, it dawned on the seeker that the teacher was simply saying that God is beyond our categories; that God is beyond definition; that our minds and our language cannot properly describe the Divine. Furthermore, he realized that anything we might say about God can be quickly negated. At that moment, a powerful realization came over the man and he became enlightened.

That teacher exhibited a deep wisdom. The enemy of spirituality is the theologian. Theologians, by nature, define and what they define they confine. It is theology which gives us dogma and doctrine - "this is true, that is false….this is correct, that is incorrect." Theology is what permits people to say "we are right, you are wrong; we are 'saved' you are not." We need to be very careful how we think about God, what we come to believe about God. We must not permit ourselves to be confined by our limited ways of understanding and speaking. The Divine is always much more than we can experience and express. God does not fit our narrowly defined concepts.

GRASPING

WHAT ARE YOU HOLDING ON TO AND WHY?

> By our attachment and our grasping,
> each one of us chooses the world we inhabit.
> **Victor M. Parachin**

Two monks lived together in a monastery for decades. They were boyhood friends. Both of them joined the monastery while in their teens. Across the years they meditated and worked side by side in the monastery. They were the best of friends and died within a few months of each other. At the moment of their rebirth, one of them was reborn as a worm in a dung pile. The other found himself in a heavenly realm having a wonderful time, enjoying the company of other enlightened beings.

His joy, however, was incomplete as he thought about his friend wondering where he had gone. So he searched his heavenly realm but could not find a trace of his beloved companion. The man then scanned the realm of humans. Again, there was no trace of his friend so he looked in the realm of animals and insects. Finally, he found him, reborn as a worm in a dung pile. His immediate thought was: "Wow, I've got to get him out of here and show him the way to the heavenly realm so he can share in my joy."

Approaching the dung pile, he called out to his mate. The little worm wriggled out saying: "Who are you?"

The old friend identified himself saying "we used to be monks together in a past life. I'm here to take you to lead you to a better place." To his amazement, the worm said: "Get lost."

With great love and patience, the worm's friend explained where he wanted to take him and how much joy he would experience there. But the worm said: "No thanks. I am quite fine right here." Desperate, the friend grabbed hold of the worm and started tugging at him. The harder he tugged, the harder the worm clung to his pile of dung.

The story ends at that point. The moral, of course, is in the form of this question: *How many of us are attached and clinging to our pile of dung?*

PS - There's one additional insight which should be considered and it's this: the two monks worshipped, meditated, worked side by side in a monastery. One was reborn to a higher, better place. The other was reborn to a lower place. How can it be that two people in the same sacred environment respond so differently?

Does this story illustrate the sad reality that some people merely become religious but not truly spiritual; that some embrace the outward form of religiosity but not the inward form of an enlightened heart?

GRATITUDE

GRATEFUL PEOPLE ARE HAPPY PEOPLE

> Gratitude is not only the greatest of virtues,
> but the parent of all others.
> Cicero

When it comes to gratitude and thankfulness, the Buddha himself is an excellent role model. On one occasion when he spoke to a group of his monks, many of whom were feeling discouraged in their journey, he said: "Let us rise up and be thankful, for if we didn't learn a lot today, at least we learned a little, and if we didn't learn a little, at least we didn't get sick, and if we got sick, at least we didn't die; so, let us all be thankful."

This simple practice is something anyone can do but very few seem to actually do it. Here is, however, an inspiring, contemporary example of someone who is doing precisely what the Buddha reminded his monks to do thousands of years ago.

A very elderly woman was living in an extended care facility. She had an unusual disease which was causing her body to slowly shut down. A young man, visiting another person at the facility, encountered this woman and continued returning to visit her. He was moved by this woman's incredible joy. Though she could no longer mover either her arms or her legs, she would joyfully and even enthusiastically tell this young man: "I am just so happy that I can move my neck." When the disease progressed and she could not move arms, legs _or_ her neck, she would say to the young man, with the same enthusiasm: "I am just so glad I can see and hear."

Because he and she had established a strong bond of friendship, the young man felt free to ask: "What would happen if you lost your sense of sound and sight?" Gently, but joyfully, she said: "I'll just be so grateful that you came to visit."

Why not find a way yourself to have the same attitude displayed by this woman and the one taught by the Buddha?

GRATITUDE – PART 2

COUNT YOUR BLESSINGS NOT YOUR BURDENS

> Let us rise up and be thankful,
> for, if we didn't learn a lot today,
> at least we learned a little, and if we didn't learn a little,
> at least we didn't get sick, and if we got sick,
> at least we didn't die; so, let us all be thankful.
> **Buddha**

Mulla Nasrudin, a sufi mystic and "holy rascal" thought to have been born in Turkey around 1208, was walking along a dusty road when he encountered a man who looked sad and despairing. "What's wrong, my brother?" asked Nasrudin. The man held up a tattered bag and moaned: "Everything I own is in this one small sack. My entire life has come down to this," he said and began to weep uncontrollably.

"That is indeed unfortunate," Nasrudin said. Then, he knocked the man down, grabbed his bag and ran down the dirt path. Shocked, the man leapt to his feet and began chasing after Nasrudin but could not catch up to him. When Nasrudin came to a bend in the path, he placed the man's sack in the middle of the road where he would come upon it. Sure enough, the man came and when he saw his back, he grabbed it with a great shout of joy. "My bag, my belongings," he cried out experiencing indescribable delight.

Watching from behind some bushes, Nasrudin chuckled and said to himself: "Well, it took so little to make him so happy."

Though this anonymous traveler's life was indeed one characterized by simplicity and poverty he worsened his life outlook by making this mistake: *he counted only his burdens but not his blessings.* It was only when he lost his blessed bag of belongings and then regained it, did he come to appreciate what he had.

This story is a poignant reminder for us to be careful how we view our lives. We can make ourselves sad, miserable, depressed, despairing, despondent and hopeless by counting up our burdens without ever acknowledging our blessings. How about you…today: *are you counting your blessings or your burdens?*

GREATNESS

WHY IT'S GREAT TO BE A HUMAN BEING

> As human beings, our greatness lies not so much in being able to remake the world - that is the myth of the 'atomic age' - as in being able to re-make ourselves.
> **Mahatma Gandhi**

An ancient tale from India tells of a rat who approached God insisting that he be turned into a human being. "They have a good life. Humans have many friends, get married, raise families, travel, learn, and have careers. I want to be a human being." God granted the rat his wish and he was re-born into the world of people. After spending many years as a human he approached God again with this request: "Please make me a rat again. Being a human being is too hard - I'm just not cut out for it."

The rat makes an interesting point. It can be challenging and frustrating to be a human being. We worry. We fear. We can feel insecure and anxious. Friends, even partners, can not only disappoint us but betray us. Humans inflict considerable violence and pain. They engage in senseless wars. The saga of human beings can indeed be a very sad one.

However, the greatness of being human is precisely what Gandhi notes, not that we can re-make the world but that we can re-make ourselves. Self transformation is always possible. Impulses for self-centeredness can give way to compassion. Anger and violence can be replaced by understanding and patience. Fear and despair can be shifted to courage and hope. *For any human being there is never a point of no return.* Anyone can change at any time. Behavioral habits which hold us back and down can be transformed. *And,* it's never too late to make a change becoming the woman or man you want to be.

H

HAPPINESS

A SIMPLE PATH TO HAPPINESS

> Whatever joy there is in this world
> All comes from desiring others to be happy,
> And whatever suffering there is in this world,
> All comes from desiring myself to be happy.
> **Shantideva**

Anyone seeking greater happiness in life can find his or her answer in this wisdom from Shantideva. Today, if you're unhappy, if you're feeling your life does not have purpose or meaning, if you feel that all you have done is drifted along, then read and re-read Shantideva's wisdom:

Whatever joy there is in this world
All comes from desiring others to be happy
And whatever suffering there is in this world
All comes from desiring myself to be happy.
But what need is there to say much more?
The childish work for their own benefit,
The Buddhas work for the benefit of others.
Just look at the difference between them!

Shantideva is one of the most highly regarded and influential teachers among Tibetan Buddhists is Shantideva. Very little is known about his life, but this much is certain:

He was an Indian Buddhist monk.

He studied and taught at Nalanda University, the premier Buddhist school of his era.

He was called "Lazybones" by other monks at Nalanda and regarded as intellectually "slow".

He is the renown author of *Guide to the Bodhisattva Way of Life* (A Bodhisattva is any individual who, motivated by compassion, is committed to achieving his or her enlightenment in order to be of benefit to others.)

According to legend, his talk was offered when students made a request for him to teach. It is believed this request was intended to embarrass Shantideva by exposing his lack of learning and force him out of the monastic university. Instead, his teaching was both profound but accessible and, today, is a major text studied by all Tibetan Buddhists. Take some time to carefully consider his wisdom. Allow Shantideva's words to imprint your mind and your heart.

HAPPINESS – PART 2

DO YOU WANT TO BE HAPPY FOR THE REST OF YOUR LIFE?

> The truth is, that no mind is much employed upon the present: recollection and anticipation fill up almost all our moments.
> **Samuel Johnson**

If you've ever asked yourself "How can I be happy" perhaps this story can offer an answer.

It is a story written by Dr. Samuel Johnson (1704-1784) who writes about a young man named Rasselas. His father is King of Abbyssinia (today's Ethopia). Unhappy, Rasselas chooses to escape his pampered and confining life as a prince and flees to a place he has heard about - the "Happy Valley." He heads there in search of happiness.

Initially, every encounter leads him to believe he has found the secret of happiness yet, upon closer examination, he leaves disillusioned. In Egypt he spends time with the party crowd. They all seem to be happy but the partying simply masquerades their problems. Next, Rasselas spends time with a wealthy landowner who, again, appears happy on first sight. Before long, however, the man confides in Rasselas telling him he lives not in happiness but in fear of his competition. Going on, Rasselas finds a hermit and begins to establish rapport with him thinking that surely an ascetic lifestyle produces contentment. That view is shattered when the hermit abruptly resolves to return to society. Rasselas further discovers that neither the married nor the single are happy observing "marriage has many pains, but celibacy has no pleasures." Finally he returns home to Abyssinia determined that there he will create his own happiness.

That's the lesson: happiness is found within, not without. And It is uncovered by living in the present moment, not longing what was nor anticipating what may come. Dr. Johnson himself wrote: "The truth is, that no mind is much employed upon the present: recollection and anticipation fill up almost all our moments." Samuel Johnson's statement echoes the advice of the Buddha: "Do not dwell in the past, do not dream of the future, concentrate the mind on the present moment."

HAPPY

IF YOU CAN DRIVE YOURSELF CRAZY

> Go confidently in the direction of your dreams.
> **Henry David Thoreau**

You can drive yourself happy!
Here's how:

Spend more time only with people who good to you and good for you.

Work less - a lot less.

Read more. Read in areas which give you pleasure - fiction, romance, self-help, spirituality, science, history, etc. The sky's the limit here. Just follow your interests.

Work in a "right livelihood" job.

Help others. Do this not out of obligation but out of compassion.

Lower your standard of living so you don't need as much income.

Nurture important relationships.

Meditate. (Yes, you have time for it. No, it's not hard to do)

Focus on the positive, not the negative. This is simply a matter of choice.

Smile more. Smile at everyone you meet. This doesn't take much effort.

Develop your spiritual and emotional side. This means grow them and mature them.

Ask 'why'? And if you don't like the answer then make the change.

Live in the present - not the past, not the future. Be here, now. Enjoy this time in your life.

These are just some ways to drive yourself happy. Add your own to the list. Then act on them!

HINDUISM

YOU MIGHT BE A HINDU IF . . .

I am proud to belong to the a religion which has taught the world both tolerance and universal acceptance.
Swami Vivekananda

You might be a Hindu (and don't know it) if you believe:

1. *There is only One God.* "Truth is One but sages call It by many names." - Rig Veda 1.164.46

2. *You respect for all religions.* "Men experience Me alone in different ways." Bhagavad Gita 4:11

3. *You see the presence of the Divine in everyone and everything.* ""He who sees all beings in the Self, and the Self in all beings, hates no one....The whole creation is filled with Divinity." Isha Upanishad 1.6.9

4. *You feel that non-violence (Ahimasa) should be a way of life.* "You must not use your God given body for killing god's creatures, whether they are human, animal or whatever." - Yajur Veda 12.32

5. *You have reverence and respect for the environment.* "The Earth is our mother, we are all Her children." - Atharva Veda 12.1.12

6. *You believe in karma – the result of our actions returns to us.* "Whatever deed he does, that he will reap." - Brihadaranyaka Upanishad 4.4.5

7. *You feel life's purpose is Self (or God) Realization.* "Lead me from unreality to reality. Lead me from darkness to light. Lead me from death to immortality." Brihadaranyaka Upanisahd 1:3.28

The above are seven foundational concepts of Hinduism. Though it is the world's oldest religion, it is amazingly current and increasingly in line with the way many are coming to believe.

HOLY BOOKS

AN ISSUE WITH HOLY BOOKS

> We should take the enlightened approach and not slavishly....resort to any holy book without using our common sense.
> **K. Shri Dhammananda**

There was once a holy man who attracted many followers, devotees. They began to record his teaching in a book and, over the years, it became their sacred text. Whenever they were uncertain about an issue, they would first consult with the book before acting.

One day they were journeying, by foot, with their teacher. While crossing a log bridge, the Master fell off into the river.

He shouted for help screaming: "I can't swim!" Rather than throw him a rope or jump into the water to help, they first opened up their holy book seeking guidance. While they did that, their master disappeared in the water and drowned.

That story is told in the East to convey this warning: "Do not become slaves to any holy book." In fact, Eastern religions view sacred texts differently than do those in the West. For example, Swami Vivekananda, a Hindu sage noted: "One peculiarity of the Vedas is that they are the only scriptures that again and again declare that you must go beyond them. The Vedas say that they were written just for the child mind; and when you have grown, you must go beyond them. "Whereas the Eastern approach is to "go beyond" any sacred scripture, Christianity – for example – locks into the bible. Their clergy often declare: "The bible says...." and that becomes the end of the issue.

Furthermore, when religious people cling too tightly to their holy book, there Swami Vivekananda says this danger emerges. "Book worship is another strong form of (religion) the strongest form. You find in every (religion) that the book becomes the God.... (Holy) books have produced more evil than good. They are accountable for many mischievous doctrines. Creeds all come from books, and books are alone responsible for the persecution and fanaticism in the world."

So, the next time someone tells you "the bible says", pause and ask yourself "so what?"

HUMILITY

BLESSED ARE THE HUMBLE

> Be humble...have no pretensions.
> **Bhagavad Gita** 13:7-8

In a small village, a Holy Man was giving a spiritual talk which was followed by a question and answer period. A wealthy merchant who was well know in the community for giving liberally to worthy causes asked: "How long will it take for me to exhaust all of my accumulated karma and achieve liberation?" Pausing only briefly, the Holy Man said that because the merchant had been an honest and honorable man it would only be 12 lifetimes before he would have a sacred vision of the Divine and experience freedom from all his karma. The merchant was pleased and thanked the Holy Man.

The next question was similar and came from a wandering ascetic who survived only by the alms he collected as well as the kindness of strangers. His question was identical to that of the wealthy merchant. The Holy man paused for a moment of meditation and answered that only three more lifetimes were required before the ascetic would experience the divine and achieve liberation.

That answer infuriated the ascetic: "Three more! That's ridiculous. After all I've sacrificed and denied myself, three more lifetimes is very unfair." The Holy Man simply responded: "That's just the way it is." With that comment, the ascetic threw away his begging bowl declaring: "In that case, I'm going to enjoy what time I have life in this life and devote myself to satisfying all my desires."

A final question came from a man known in the community as one recently released from prison. He'd spent most of his adult life in various jails and had many convictions. He also asked how long it would take for "someone like me to exhaust all of my accumulated karma and achieve liberation?" The Holy Man pointed to a nearby enormous tree saying: "Look at that tree. As many leaves as there on that tree, so many lives it will take for you to work out your karma." With that answer, the ex-convict began to weep and dance with joy shouting so everyone could hear: "How compassionate is God! After all the wrong things I've done

God still gives me a change to reach Him, and it will only take that many lifetimes. Oh, how fortunate I am!"

At that very moment, the Divine emerged from the sky granting him freedom and liberation right on the spot. It was the man's humility and deep gratitude which brought him this surprising turn of events. As you go through this week remember the words of the Bhagavad Gita: "Be humble..have no pretensions."

HURRY

HURRY UP AND SLOW DOWN!

> Nature does not hurry;
> yet, everything is accomplished.
> **Lao Tzu**

Pause for a moment to think about the answer to this question: *Why are people not more compassionate?*

Some would answer that people are naturally unkind and insensitive. I don't like that response because it suggests that human beings are inherently calloused and compassion-less. The fact is that many times people act without compassion simply because they're in a hurry. People rush to drop their kids off at child care. They rush to work. At the end of the day they rush to pick their children up and race home. Then there are chores to do and errands to run in the evenings and weekend. It's all hurry, hurry, and hurry with very little space for compassion. That's one conclusion which can be drawn from this classic experiment in social psychology done in the 1970s by John Darley and Daniel Batson.

They recruited 67 students from Princeton Theological Seminary explaining they were conducting a study about people who enter religious professions. The Seminary students were asked to fill in some personality questionnaires. As part of the study the students were told they would also to go to other campus classrooms at Princeton University to talk about the parable of the "Good Samaritan" (This was a story Jesus told about a man who had been robbed, beaten and left wounded on the ground. Three people walked by the poor man but only one stopped to help him.)

Here's where the experiment gets interesting. Unknown to the seminary students, an actor had been hired to pretend he was in pain. The actor was on the ground with eyes closed, coughing and moaning. All the seminary students would have to pass right by the distressed man. The question: would they stop to help him? The students were divided into three groups. The first group we're told, after finishing the questionnaire, "You're late for the talk. They were expecting you a few minutes ago. You'd better get going." The second group we're told that a teaching assistant "is ready for you, so please go right over." The last group we're informed: "It will be a few minutes before they're ready for you, but you might as well head on over." Effectively, the experimenters created three conditions: high, medium and low hurry people. Here are the results:

High hurry group – only 10% stopped to help.

Medium hurry group – only 45% stopped to help

Low hurry group – 63% stopped to help.

This is an amazing study, one which conveys this powerful insight: *To increase compassion all we need to do is hurry up and slow down.* We need to structure our day and the events of our day in such a way that we are not racing from one place to another, from one activity to another and from one person to another. When we're not pressed and stressed, there is time for compassion.

HUMILITY

WHY HUMILITY IS SO IMPORTANT

> Humility, very simply, is the absence of arrogance. Where there is no arrogance, you relate with your world as an eye-level situation, without one-upmanship.
> **Trungpa**

As the news of a highly respected and much loved teacher swept through villages in the area, many came by his simple home to pay their last respects and honor this esteemed teacher. One by one they stood at his bedside, extolling his many contributions. He smiled weakly and listened carefully. "You have extended us so much kindness," said one devotee. Another lamented "Your skill as a teacher cannot be replicated." Yet another thanked him saying "Your depth of knowledge has been both impressive and personally inspiring."

Many other tributes were spoken about his wisdom, compassion, patience and eloquence. These continued until his wife observed signs of restlessness and kindly explained to his devotees he was too weak for visitors. Turning to her husband, she asked why he was agitated reminding him every visitor brought a wonderful tribute to him. "Yes, it was all wonderful," he whispered, "but did you notice that no one mentioned my humility?"

Of course, the very fact he raised this issue indicates that he was able to tame his ego. Nevertheless, he was wise to be concerned because pride in our work and activities can easily slip into arrogance if it is not disciplined. Conceit can masquerade itself as humility and pride. Such conceit is always and simply self-deceit. This good man needed assurance he had not slipped into that mode. He was aware that an over inflated ego has the power to distort compassion into it's very opposite, pity; that an unchecked ego disables our capacity to learn from others.

That's why modern Buddhist teacher Chogyam Trungpa says: "Humility, very simply, is the absence of arrogance. Where there is no arrogance, you relate with your world as an eye-level situation, without one-upmanship. Because of that, there can be a genuine interchange." When true humility is present, he adds that "nobody is using their message to put anybody else down, and nobody has to come down or up to the other person's level. Everything is eye-level."

Here are some signs of a humble spirit. Compare your style to this short list:

Humility means:

Being willing to put others first;

Not building yourself up by pulling others down;

Acknowledging weakness, errors, mistakes, poor judgments;

Ability to see personal liabilities and abilities in balanced ways;

Listening to others;

Receiving advice from other people;

Admitting and owning hurtful actions even when they were unintentional;

Never gloating or criticizing when proven to have been right.

IDIOT COMPASSION

NOT ALL COMPASSIONS ARE EQUAL

> Compassion must be linked
> with skillful action.
> **Victor M. Parachin**

Entertain, for a moment, the idea that not all compassions are equal nor is every compassionate act truly helpful. For example, a woman in her 30s was recently arrested and jailed. While driving drunk during the mid afternoon, she ran over and killed 2 bicyclists. As news reporters investigated further, they learned the woman had been jailed two other times for driving while drunk. On both of those previous occasions, a family member promptly bailed her out of jail and paid for her legal defense. She was driving again on probation.

Consider also a letter written to an advice columnist from a young woman: "I'm desperate for guidance. I have no mentors to consult nor anyone with more life experience because I have no family left I can talk to anymore." She went on to explain that, five years earlier, her father ended his life by suicide in front of the woman and her mother. "His family blamed me for not trying to wrestle the loaded gun from him." His side of the family ended the relationship with the young woman and her mother. After that, the mother began drinking heavily. "Mom loses jobs for being drunk, is all but black-listed in the city she lives in and is often short of rent money." The daughter has given her money to pay living expenses but she "blows it on alcohol." The young woman ended her letter saying "I know picking her up only enable her drinking. Please help me. I don't know what to do."

In Tibetan Buddhism there is the concept of "Idiot Compassion" and it would apply to both these cases. In the first one – the woman driving after drinking - family member was not helpful in posting bail and paying legal fees. The result, she continued to drink and drive killing two innocent people. In the second situation, the young woman's own emotional well-being would be adversely impacted if she did not distance herself from her mother. In fact, the advice columnist said: "It is extremely important for your emotional well-being to let go of your guilt for being unable to mother your mother. You are a caring and dutiful daughter, but the burden you have assumed will crush you if you don't put it down. No one can save someone who doesn't want to be saved."

Compassion must always be tightly linked to wisdom and skillful action. When that isn't the case, then idiot compassion takes place. Here are some ways of recognizing idiot compassion. It is evident: when

we hinder rather than help;

we enable rather than disable;

we feel better, less distressed;

we give to get;

we act but with an agenda;

we don't have the courage to say 'no'.

It's safe to say that most of us have been in the situation of trying to help a family member or friend who is in some kind of difficulty. We suggest changes, offer advice, network on their behalf only to see the friend or family member repeating the same negative pattern over and over. Then we try to do more, push and prod more to get the result _we're_ seeking. Basically we're not doing what they need, _but what we need._ Idiot compassion is merely a way of easing our feelings - "I just can't bear to see him suffer". So we practice idiot compassion as way of helping ourselves.

Chogyam Trungpa, a prominent Tibetan Buddhist teacher bluntly says: "Idiot compassion, which is compassion with neurosis, is a slimy way of trying to fulfill your desire secretly. This is your aim, but you give the appearance of being generous and impersonal."

ILLUSION

THE REALITY OF ILLUSION.

> First appearances deceive many.
> **Ovid**

Many years ago a man was traveling on foot through the rural Indian countryside. When he arrived at a small village, a kind resident invited him to spend the night in his modest hut. In the middle of the night, the man awakened and saw a deadly snake coiled next to his legs on the bed. The man was terrified because he knew the area was inhabited by many poisonous snakes. He also knew that, if bitten, there was no clinic anywhere in the region and he would surely die before aid could be administered. He spent the night paralyzed with fear and terrified of moving for fear of startling the snake. As the sun emerged and filled his room with light he discovered that the coiled "snake" was actually his own belt which he left on the bed.

There are times when our perception is actually misperception. This simple story can teach us in at least two ways. First, we can think of times when our first impression was absolutely wrong and from that experience we ought to know better than to make harsh judgments based on one encounter. Secondly, we can think of times when we were victimized by someone else's perception of us. Some act or words of ours, intended innocently enough, were perceived in a completely different and hostile way. In actuality we were merely a "belt" but were seen as a dangerous coiled "snake." The wise among us know that what we see is not always accurate and therefore we must work harder to discipline our vision.

ILLUSION – PART 2

CHALLENGING OUR ILLUSIONS

There are as many pillows of illusion as flakes in a snow-storm. We wake from one dream into another dream.
Ralph Waldo Emerson

Check out a dictionary definition of "illusion" and you will find these descriptions: *an erroneous mental representation; deception by creating illusory ideas; an erroneous perception of reality; a condition of being deceived by a false perception or belief.* Because illusions are ever present, creeping and growing like weeds in a garden, we must be on guard at all times to challenge them _or_ recognize when someone else shatters an illusion we live by. Consider this story about a highly respected spiritual teacher who once encountered a very wealthy man in his community. The man proudly described to the spiritual master his lifestyle which was extremely ascetic. "I eat only one meal a day and it consists of dry bread, salt and water." To his astonishment, the spiritual master responded: "You are a fool!" Then, he instructed the wealthy man to "go home and eat fine delicacies, rich meat and drink aged wine. If you don't, you will hear more from me!"

Later, followers of the spiritual master asked why he spoke that way. Their teacher explained: "If the rich man dines on meat and wine, then he would at least feel that the poor in his town should be given bread and salt. But if he himself subsists on dry bread, salt and water, he might feel that poor people could live on stone." The spiritual master was challenging a powerful illusion in the life of the wealthy man. In adopting the ascetic lifestyle and eating only dry bread, salt and water he could easily tell himself, "If I can do this, so can the poor." However, what he misses is the fact that he has a choice of his lifestyle. The poor have no choice. They can only eat dry bread, salt and water. So, the spiritual master was quite right: the wealthy man's ascetic lifestyle simply created another illusion why he did not need to help the poor. If that wealthy individual was wise, he would appreciate the teacher's challenge to his illusion.

Look more closely at your life. Be on the lookout for illusions - erroneous perceptions of reality - which may cloud your life. Remain sensitive to others who may come into your life challenging those illusions.

ILLUSION – PART 3

THE BLACK NOSED BUDDHA

> Illusion is the first of all pleasures.
> **Voltaire**

A nun who was searching for enlightenment made a statue of Buddha. Though it was already elegant, she then covered it with gold leaf. Wherever she went she carried this golden Buddha with her. The statue reminded her of whom she wanted to become.

Years passed and, still carrying her Buddha, the nun came to live in a small temple in a country where there were many Buddhas, each one with its own particular shrine. The nun wished to burn incense before her golden Buddha but didn't like the idea of the incense smoke straying to the others. So, she devised a funnel through which the smoke would ascend only to her statue. This blackened the nose of the golden Buddha, making it especially ugly.

How odd is this story that a woman on a spiritual path seeking enlightenment could act in such an unenlightened way. It raises these kinds of interesting questions: *How common is this in our culture? How commonly do we see this in others around us? How common is this in our own lives? How could she - and anyone else - be so unaware of their self-negating behavior?* Voltaire's insight is worthy of further personal reflection: "Illusion is the first of all pleasures."

IMPERFECTION

EMBRACING IMPERFECTION

> This is the very perfection of a man,
> to find out his own imperfections.
> **St. Augustine**

A young priest was placed in charge of the garden within a famous Zen temple. He had been given the job because he was a natural: he loved flowers, shrubs, trees and all growing things. Behind the fence and in a small hut lived a very old Zen master. One day the young priest learned that important visitors were coming to the temple. That day he took extra care in tending to the garden. He pulled weeds, trimmed the shrubs, combed the moss, raked the sandy area and spend a great deal of time meticulously raking up and disposing all of the dry autumn leaves.

As he worked, the old master watched him with amused interest from across the wall which separated his hut from the garden area. When the young priest was finished, he stood back admiring his work and said to the old master: "Isn't this beautiful!" The old master said "Yes, but there is something missing. Help me over this wall and I'll make the correction for you."

Not sure what the old master was referring to, the young priest hesitatingly helped lift the older man over the wall placing him in the garden area. Slowly, the master walked to the tree near the center of the garden, grabbed it by the trunk shaking it. Drying fall leaves began to shower down all over the garden. "There," said the old Zen master, "you can put me back now."

Through that action, the master was trying to teach the young priest about the importance of embracing and even welcoming imperfection. Life is seldom perfect. If we expect that, we only set ourselves up for disappointment and suffering. Furthermore, our greatest opportunities for growth to occur when we are "imperfect" - when we fail, err, blunder, make mistakes, and blow it. Most people identify their own life growth points as coming when things were far from perfect: a loved one dies, a friend disappoints, a diagnosis of illness is given, a divorce takes place, a disabling sickness emerges. We can become sad and mad but the wise ones among use the imperfect times of our lives to grow, to see and sense life at a deeper level. It is in those "imperfect" moments that the capacity of our heart is enlarged making us kinder, gentler, more compassionate people.

Embracing imperfection is something often done by artists such as weavers and potters who deliberately create a flaw in their work. They do this as a way of saying there is no such thing as perfection in any human endeavor. Therefore, rather that become frustrated with events which are less than perfect, they invite us to embrace imperfection because it has a type of beauty of its own. Today, reflect on the wisdom of Augustine's words: *This is the very perfection of a man, to find out his own imperfections.*

IMPERMANENCE

LIFE IS ALWAYS IN MOTION

> Life is like a river, always flowing.
> **Victor M. Parachin**

An ancient story tells about a king who knew he would soon die so he called his three sons to his bedside, one by one. To first one he said: "You are my oldest son so I am giving you my kingdom. May you govern faithfully and justly." To the second one he said: "You are my middle son. I am giving you all of my estates. May you run them wisely so that the harvest will be abundant and the people on them may prosper." Finally, he called on his third and youngest son, who was also his favorite. "To you most beloved," the father said, "I give you what has been most precious and important in my life." He handed his son a ring. On the inside were inscribed these four words: *This too shall pass.* Though some might feel his youngest was short changed, the king was really giving the young man something more important and powerful than his kingdom or his estates. He was transmitting the wisdom that life is impermanent; that nothing stays the same for very long. Awareness of this reality could help his son triumph over any and every adversity which might come into his life.

This is something we need to remember whenever we face a painful challenge. It can help to remind ourselves that the reality is that no crisis lasts forever. Nothing in life remains the same for very long. *This too shall pass* is wisdom telling us that we simply need to deal with life as best we can on day-to-day basis working for the best possible outcome. We do that knowing that the moment _will_ come when the dilemma eases and things change for the better. Life is like a river, always flowing. It is impermanent.

IMPERMANENCE – PART 2

CHANGE IS INEVITABLE: GET USED TO IT!

> Life begins at the end of your comfort zone.
> **Neale Donald Walsch**

In Buddhist thought impermanence is the undeniable reality that change is inevitable. In fact, Buddhism notes that everything on our planet is subject to change. Rivers change. Lakes change. Even the mountains change. And, change will come to every single person. Some changes are welcome but many are not. Much of our suffering results from our inability or unwillingness to adjust our lives to the change which has come. When change comes we suffer more deeply when we cling to the way we wish our lives were rather than adapt to the way it really is.

Because change is inevitable, it is crucial for us to view change with the eye of an optimist. Rather than fear and loathe an unwelcome change, we can train ourselves to embrace it by viewing it in these ways:

Change comes to everyone.

Change is an opportunity for personal growth.

Change brings new opportunities, new people, new perspectives.

Change nudges us to become more flexible and resilient.

Change creates new patterns of thinking and viewing life.

Change enables us to learn important lessons.

Change is a reminder we are not always in control.

Change helps us surrender or relinquish control.

Change empowers us to tap into our Higher Self.

Change gives me a choice in how I will respond.

Change develops and deepens my personality.

Change heightens inner strength and resolve.

Change provides me with an opportunity to regroup and rebuild.

Change can be good.

IMPROVEMENT

7 TIPS TO IMPROVE YOUR SPIRITUAL LIFE

> Let us strive to improve ourselves,
> for we cannot remain stationary;
> one either progresses or retrogrades.
> **Marie Anne de Vichy-Chamrond**

Right action is fourth on the Buddha's eightfold path. It is a call to spiritual and ethical self-improvement. Here are 7 tips to improve your spiritual life:

1. Serve. Be of help and encouragement to others. Service is foundational for a healthy spiritual life. A German university student who lost his faith visited with theologian Karl Rahner asking what books he might read to recover it. Rahner advised the student not to read books but to "go and serve the poor in Munich and your faith will be rekindled."

2. Meditate. "Be still and know that I am God," is the teaching of Psalm 46:10. Silence and stillness are tools to enlarge the spirit. Thomas Merton observed: "It is in deep solitude and silence that I find the gentleness with which I

can truly love my brother and sister." The Buddha bluntly stated: "Meditation brings wisdom; lack of meditation brings ignorance. Know well what leads you forward and what holds you back and choose the path that leads to wisdom."

3. Utter blessings. Wherever you move during the day, offer silent blessings upon everyone you encounter. Say to yourself, "May you be richly blessed" as you deal with a bank teller, a retail clerk, an office receptionist, work colleagues, people in the elevator, your family and so on. Utter blessings on the difficult people you encounter as well.

4. Live in the present moment. Don't permit yourself to be dragged down by regrets from yesterday or fear of the future. Remember the wisdom of the psalm writer who declared: "Today is the day the Lord has made, let us rejoice and be glad in it." (Psalm 118:24) Spiritual writer Iyanla Vanzant advises: "Do not allow yesterday's garbage to influence your experience today. Don't allow fears about tomorrow's garbage to steal the goodness available to you right now."

5. Partner with others. Going it alone can be tough and discouraging. Joining with others who are on a spiritual path can be motivating, inspiring, and expanding. Find a group of people who share your spiritual vision and join with them: a congregation, meditation group, prayer circle, bible study class, choir, etc. In his book, Returning: A Spiritual Journey, Dan Wakefield tells of returning to a church after decades of absence. He writes: "Going to church, even belonging to it, did not solve life's problems...but it gave me a sense of living in a larger context, of being part of something greater than what I could see through the tunnel vision of my personal concerns."

6. Get outdoors. People don't fully realize how much of an outdoor, nature book the bible is. Jesus often referred to the natural world to drive home spiritual lessons: "Look at the birds of the air..." (Matthew 6:26); "See how the lilies of the field grow..." (Matthew 6:29). Psalm writers were nurtured by nature: "He makes me to lie down in green pastures; he leads me beside quiet waters." (Psalm 23:2) Be like Jesus and the Psalmists: get outdoors. Spend time in nature and ponder the wonder on the planet.

7. Disable discouragement. Don't permit discouragement to get the upper hand. Developing a healthy spiritual life has its ups and downs. Let yourself be guided by this wisdom from Rabbi Nachman of Breslov: "Don't be frustrated by the obstacles you encounter on your spiritual journey. They are there by design, to increase your desire for the goal you seek. Because the greater your goal, the greater the yearning you'll need to achieve it."

INTERCONNECTEDNESS

BENEFICIAL OR HARMFUL

We cannot live only for ourselves. A thousand fibers connect
us with our fellow men; and among those fibers, as
sympathetic threads, our actions run as causes, and they come
back to us as effects.
Herman Melivlle

Many centuries ago in China there was a drought which extended for several years. This brought great misery and hardship to a small province which depended on heavy rains to produce rice and other crops. As dry years passed, the reserves of rice dwindled to nothing. The elderly, the young and the ill began to die from starvation.

Desperate, the villagers began to implore the spirits of ancestors to influence the weather. They performed long abandoned rituals hoping to stir whatever spirits or gods controlled rain. They weren't really sure these rituals would work, but they were desperate. The rain was needed.

Finally, just when the province was about to be completely devastated and turned into an inhabitable desert, the rains came and came and came. Day after day, it rained and the rice seedling thrived in the flooded paddies. The crop that season was the biggest in memory.

A sage in the community brought this matter to the attention of his student and disciple asking: "Do you think that the rains were truly beneficial?"

"It would seem that they were," the students answered.

"So it would seem" the Sage responded but added: "The neighboring province, whose villages were all situated along the banks of several rivers, experienced the worst flash floods of their history this season. The water came pouring suddenly down steep canyons and washed whole villages away, killing hundreds of men, women and children. What do you suppose their view of the rainy season might have been?"

"That it was most harmful," said the student.

Here's the question for us: *what is the Sage trying to teach his student?* There are a couple of possible answers. First, he is reminding the disciple that nature is neutral. It does not favor one province but condemn another. It is what it is. Therefore people need to be careful about crediting or blaming God for nature's activity. There is modern parallel to this ancient story. I live in a state which is part of 'tornado alley'. Tornadoes strike this state many times every year. And, each year there will be someone on a local news station who says: "God saved us from the tornado." However, what does it say about God when that person's neighbor was not spared; when there was loss of life and property caused by the same tornado? Neither God nor nature sends earthquakes, floods, tsunamis etc.

Secondly, and perhaps more importantly, the Sage was teaching his student about the interconnectedness of life. What was beneficial for one province was a disaster for the other. The appropriate response of the people benefiting from the rain would be humility saying among themselves: "We were fortunate but our neighboring sisters and brothers suffer." And then, they should work to provide relief for those in need.

INVENTORY

ASSESSING YOUR WEALTH

> Poverty and wealth originate in the mind.
> **Victor M. Parachin**

A man who was happily married and had prospered greatly had a son whom he loved very much. When his son was seven the father took him on trip into the countryside where they stayed with a poor family in a small village. The father's intent was to show his son how poor people live so that the son would not take his privileged life for granted but appreciate what he had. As they returned home, the father asked his son what he thought about their excursion. Here's the way their conversation flowed:

"The trip was wonderful, father."

"Did you see how poor people live?" the father asked.

"Yes, I did!"

"Well, then, what did you learn from our trip?" inquired the father.

The son replied: "I saw that we have one dog and they had four. We have a pool that reaches to the middle of our garden, and they have a creek which has no end. We have imported lantern in our garden, and they have stars at night. Our patio reaches to the front yard, and they have the whole horizon. We have a small piece of land to live on, and they have fields that go beyond our sight. We have servants who serve us, they serve one another. We buy our food but they grow theirs. We have walls around our property to protect us; they have friends to protect them. So, I thank you father for showing me how poor we are!"

Poverty and wealth originate in the mind. Are you wealthy or poor?

J

JOY

REJOICING IN THE JOY OF OTHERS

> Thoughts give joy when they speak or act.
> Joy follows them like a shadow
> which never leaves them.
> **Buddha**

In her book, *Awakening The Kind Heart,* Kathleen McDonald tells of visiting Varanasi, a city in Northern India famous for its many temples and religious festivals. She arrived at her hotel around 9 pm quite weary and was dismayed to hear the air filled with Indian Pop Music blaring. A wedding party was being held in the courtyard of the hotel. Her heart sank as thoughts of a good night's sleep began to evaporate.

Even in her room, the music permeated the walls and was so loud it was impossible to concentrate on anything. As negative feelings began to take over her mind, she remembered a story one of her spiritual teachers had shared. he also was in a similar situation. Across the street from his monastery was a hotel which was hosting an all night wedding party. But, in his case, the loud music did not annoy him because he began to rejoice in the happiness of the people at the party: the bride, the bridegroom, the attendants, the families and friends.

McDonald decided to adopt his approach and begin to rejoice in the joy of all those involved with the wedding. She sat down and in a meditative state envisioned what a joyous occasion this was for the couple, their family and friends. Rather quickly, she began to share in their joy and sent loving kindness their way wishing them happiness as well as love and compassion for each other for the rest of their lives. McDonald found this simple exercise of rejoicing in others' joy transformed her mind. The music was no longer an irritant.

This is a principle which more people can and ought to adopt in daily life. Why not rejoice in the joy young people skateboarding along a sidewalk? Why not rejoice in the joy of a couple in love and walking hand in hand? Why not rejoice when a work colleague receives an important promotion?

JOY - PART 2

TIME TO LIGHTEN UP

> Let us live most happily, possessing nothing;
> let us feed on joy, like the radiant gods.
> **The Dhammapada** 15:4

A Tibetan master was brought to a meditation center in Minneapolis, Minnesota where he would teach and lead meditation. Initially he was impressed with the zealousness and sincerity of the American meditators. However, he quickly noticed that the meditators were far too serious. No one smiled. No one laughed. Their practice was serious business, too serious the Tibetan monk. During some free time, he went shopping in Minneapolis where he purchased a toy water pistol. At the next meditation session, he began to squirt the zealous meditators with his water gun. Of course eyes would peek open during meditation to see where the water was coming from. When they saw their master teacher squirting them with a water pistol, they began to smile. Before long they were chuckling and then laughing out loud.

Spirituality is a serious task, or so most people seem to think. Spiritual endeavors are done by many of us with discipline and firmness. Engaging ourselves in the spiritual means being somber, solemn, stern and even severe with ourselves. The truth is, we take this matter far too seriously. When we're too serious about this matter, we become uptight, impatient, and easily frustrated. There's also a danger of becoming self-righteous. The greater truth is that pursuing a spiritual path should be done with a smile on our face, lightness in our spirits and joy in our hearts. That's the intent of the quote from the Dhammapada, a collection of the Buddha's sayings. *Let us live most happily, possessing nothing; let us feed on joy, like the radiant gods.*

K

KARMA

DEALING WITH HUNGRY BEARS

> They sow the wind and reap the whirlwind.
> **Hosea** 8:7

A naturalist living above the tree line in northern Canada had a companion dog. Whenever he let the dog outdoors, he made sure the dog was properly tethered to a stake he had driven into the ground. Early one spring day, the man looked out the window to see a polar bear walking toward his dog. The polar bear had obviously emerged from a winter of hibernation and was very, very hungry. The man watched in terror as the bear approached his dog. He was certain the bear would attack and devour his companion.

Then, something completely unexpected took place. The dog did not see a predator but a playmate. As the bear approached, the dog began to wag its tail, crouch into the snow and yelp with pleasure at meeting a playmate and greeting a new friend. In spite of being ravenous, the bear responded to the dog in the friendliest ways. The bear dropped onto the ground playfully tossing snow at the dog. For a few moments, the dog and the bear lay on the ground, nose to nose before the bear began to roll around on the snow entertaining his new friend. At one point, the bear, while laying on its back, took the dog into its arms giving the dog a huge bear hug. Though the man was astonished by what he was witnessing, he quickly reached for his camera taking pictures which were later published in a nature magazine. Over the next several days, the bear returned to play with his new friend.

There is an important lesson for us to observe from the encounter of this charming incident. By being open, friendly, inviting, playful, the dog completely disarmed the hungry bear. Imagine how that incident could have totally different had the dog begun to be aggressive and hostile. This is a karmic law: the energy we send out is the same energy which turns back to us or upon us. Good actions and intentions reap good rewards; bad actions and intentions result in suffering and pain. Specifically, when we exhibit warmth and kindness, we will receive the same from others. Conversely, when we exude frustration and anger, that turns upon us as well.

Perhaps this story can guide us the next time we must deal with "hungry bear" who comes into our life. Perhaps the words of the Jewish prophet Hosea can offer us a caution: *They sow the wind and reap the whirlwind.* The prophet succinctly issues this warning: "Think before you act. Everything you do has consequences. The priorities you hold in life have consequences. The choices you make have consequences."

KINDNESS

TRAIN YOUR MIND TO BE KIND

> The smallest act of kindness is worth
> more than the grandest intention.

Buddhist teacher Jack Kornfield tells of being with two journalist friends who interviewed the Dalai Lama for a radio program. The Dalai Lama is understandably very busy as leader of Tibetan Buddhists and as leader of the Tibetan government in exile. Nevertheless, he greeted Kornfield and his colleagues warmly even serving them tea himself. With great patience and no indication of being in a hurry, he answered all of their questions and when it was evident they were through, the Dalai Lama asked: "Is there anything else I could do for you?" They said "no" not wanting to take more of his time but the Dalai Lama asked: "Don't you want to take my picture?"

Actually all three of them brought cameras but in the excitement of the interview forgot about them. The Dalai Lama suggested they give their three cameras to his aide so that all of them could pose with the Dalai Lama. Centered between them the Dalai Lama placed his arms around them smiling broadly.

After the photos were taken, the Dalai Lama grasped Kornfield by the hand and turned to him. Since Kornfield and the Dalai Lama knew each other, Kornfield was sure the Tibetan leader was going to ask him about his work teaching meditation. Instead however, he simply squeezed Kornfield's hand, looked at him carefully and said: "You're so skinny. You should eat more!"

Look closely at that entire story and note that, moment by moment, the Dalai Lama extended kindness. The lesson: no one is too important or too busy to be kind. Kindness is a great blessing which is was Kornfield experienced.

KRISHNA

WISDOM FROM KRISHNA

Krishna insisted on outer cleanliness and inner cleansing.
Clean clothes and clean minds are an ideal combination
Sri Sathyia Sai Baba

Krishna, one of India's most revered and respected deities, is
the speaker of the *Bhagavad-gita*. Krishna is as revered to
Hindus as Christ is to Christians. Some suggest that they are
the same noting the similarity of names: Krishna and Christ.
In the Bhagarad-gita, Krishna offers spiritual advice and
counsel to a warrior named Arjuna. Here are some gems of
wisdom via Krishna which can guide us today:

He alone sees truly who sees the Lord the same in every
creature...seeing the same Lord everywhere, he does not
harm himself or others.

No one should abandon duties because he sees defects in
them. Every action, every activity, is surrounded by defects
as a fire is surrounded by smoke.

Even though scolded by the wicked or insulted, ridiculed,
calumniated, beaten, bound, robbed of his living or spat upon
or otherwise abominably treated by the ignorant-being thus
variously shaken and placed in dire extremities, the man who
desires his well-being should deliver himself by his own
efforts through patience and non-resistance.

The awakened sages call a person wise when all his undertakings are free from anxiety about results.

Be fearless and pure; never waver in your determination or your dedication to the spiritual life. Give freely. Be self-controlled, sincere, truthful, loving, and full of the desire to serve...Learn to be detached and to take joy in renunciation. Do not get angry or harm any living creature, but be compassionate and gentle; show good will to all. Cultivate vigor, patience, will, purity; avoid malice and pride. Then, you will achieve your destiny.

Reshape yourself through the power of your will... Those who have conquered themselves...live in peace, alike in cold and heat, pleasure and pain, praise and blame...To such people a clod of dirt, a stone, and gold are the same...Because they are impartial, they rise to great heights.

L

LEADERS

HOT TUB LESSON

> Get rid of the self and act from The Self.
> **Zen Proverb**

Many centuries ago in a small Japanese village there were two Buddhist temples. This tiny village was declining in population and the 60 remaining families could no longer afford to support both temples. One had to be closed so the other could be properly supported. The villagers decided to find a way of determining which of the two temple priests was more suited to be their spiritual leader. One was a monk and the other was priest.

So they set up a test or contest and promoted it in their village. On the day of the testing, all the villagers gathered in the village center where they had set up a large tub of boiling water. They asked the two priests, "What would you do with this tub of boiling water?"

The monk stepped forward first. He was a tall, well built man, the result of the long hard training required by his school. He stepped up to the tub and recited several sacred mantras followed by hand gestures (called mudras) which focused his mind. Slowly he lowered himself into the boiling water. It was an impressive sight. The boiling water did not seem to affect the monk in any way as he calmly lowered all the way down until his shoulders were completely immersed. Villagers looked on in awe and amazement as he stepped out of the tub without any visible signs of being scalded or harmed.

Now the villagers turned to the other man, the priest, repeating their question, "What would you do with this tub of boiling water?" He turned to the villagers asking them to bring several more large wooden tubs filled halfway with cold water. Though the villagers thought this was a strange request, they did as he asked. When the additional tubs arrived, the priest began pouring hot water from the boiling vat into the tubs to make them lukewarm. Then he said: "This is perfect for a hot tub soak but it's a waste for me to enjoy this all by myself. Why don't all of you join me and, together, let us enjoy hot tubing." The villagers began to smile at his invitation and most of them joined him. Appreciating the warm water, a camaraderie developed with several leading the others in singing. Everyone had a great time.

Now it was decision time. On the one hand, the villagers were impressed with the monk's near super human abilities but they wondered what use those abilities were to them and to their children. On the other hand, the priest displayed no such powers. However, he seemed like one of them *and* he lived by ideals of sharing, humility, and finding extraordinary joy in ordinary things. His life could be modeled and practiced by everyone in the village. It proved to be an easy decision and the priest was invited to be the village spiritual leader.

There are a couple of ways to apply this story. First, it's worth asking yourself about the spiritual leaders or writers who shape your life. Are they like the monk or the priest? If they are like the monk - simply out to impress - can you make a self-correction and look for spiritual leaders and writers who are more like the priest; those whose lives inspire you to model and live out their values.

Secondly, try making this story your own personal story. Ask yourself this urgent question: *Is my personality, my spirituality, cultivated and developed to impress people or to inspire people?* Reflect on this Zen proverb: "Get rid of the self and act from The Self."

LESSON

A JAR AND SOME ROCKS

> Sorting out what's important and what's not will keep your life from becoming trivial and unimportant.
> **Victor M. Parachin**

At a prominent American business school where students were all working toward an MBA (Master of Business Administration) degree, a professor came into class with a glass jar. Without explaining what he was doing, the professor placed the jar on his desk. Then, in view of the students, he brought out a bag full of stones and carefully placed them one by one into the jar until no more would go in. He asked the students: "Is the jar full?"

"Yes," they replied in unison.

The professor smiled. From beneath the desk he produced a second bag, this one full of coarse gravel. He then managed to shake the gravel into the spaces between the larger stones. A second time he asked: "Is the jar full?"

Not wanting to be tricked again, they said, "No."

That was the correct answer because, for the third time, the professor produced a bag of very fine sand. He managed to coax a lot of the fine powdery sand into the spaces between the stones and the coarse gravel. So, he asked again, "Is the jar full?"

Smiling, the students said, "Probably not!"

The professor smiled back and brought out a small jug of water which poured into the jar full of stones, coarse gravel and fine sand. When the water reached the top rim of the glass filling it completely, he asked:

"So, what does this simple demonstration teach you?" he asked the class.

One student responded: "No matter how busy your schedule you can always fit something more in!"

"No" said the professor directly and bluntly. "It's about priorities! If you want to get the big stones in, you have to put then in _first!_"

He was delivering this lesson to his MBA students: the "big stones" in your life are your most important priorities. Ensure that they are placed into your life – symbolized by the empty jar – first and before other things are put in leaving little or not room for the "precious stones" of their lives.

Priorities are so important that, in the Buddhist tradition, people are often asked to meditate on death. "Living with the immediacy of death helps you sort out your priorities in life. It helps you to live a less trivial life" notes Sogyal Rinpoche. When proper priorities are not established, then life becomes unbalanced, unfulfilled and unhappy.

LIBERATION

LIBERATING OURSELVES
FROM OUR INHUMANITY

> The moment one gives close attention to
> anything, even a blade of grass, it becomes
> a mysterious, awesome, indescribably
> magnificent world in itself.
> **Henry Miller**

A group of spice traders were making their way across China where they encountered a Buddhist monastery. They stopped at the monastery for food and rest. Inside the monastery they heard a commotion coming from the main hall. Out of curiosity they peeked through the door to see what was going on. To their astonishment they saw people screaming, shouting, shaking. The scene reminded them of insane asylums they had heard about. They concluded the hall was filled with people who were being held and treated for insanity. Throughout all that chaos, however, the Master of the monastery was sitting calmly and silently. The spice traders understood that monasteries were places where people came to seek and find enlightenment. But in this case, the Master seemed only to have attracted students who suffered from insanity. They also concluded the Master was not in control of the group since he sat quietly in meditation, almost oblivious to the chaos going on all around him. The traders departed shaking their heads in disbelief.

Three months later the same travelers passed by the monastery. Out of curiosity they looked into the main hall expecting to see the severely mentally ill. To their astonishment they saw the very same people but, this time, very orderly and sitting quietly in meditation. In contrast to their first visit the transformation was miraculous. Again, the traders departed shaking their heads in disbelief.

As their route was one regularly traveled by those who traded, the same group passed by the monastery three months later. Recalling the last two visits, they were curious about the monastery residents. Quietly making their way to the great hall, the peered in and now found to their surprise that no one was screaming and no one was meditation. The place was vacant. Only the monastery master was present sitting there in meditation. Their curiosity was so great they entered the main hall speaking with the master:

"What has happened here?" they asked. "Months ago when we first visited, people were screaming, shouting, shaking as if they were insane? But on our second visit those very same people were calm and in meditation. Now we have returned a third time and no one is here. What has happened?"

"There is a simple explanation," said the Master: "When you first passed by the monastery was filled with novices who brought with them the madness and insanity of the world. I encouraged them to experience and purge the pain they had absorbed by simply being alive. The second time you passed by, they had become more settled and were in meditation quietly listening and exploring their inner selves and seeking to connected with their greater Selves. By your third visit they have all returned to their home cities, towns and villages to share their new awareness and to facilitate the transformation of their communities toward a more humane way of living. At this moment I am waiting for the arrival of a new group of novices. When you pass by the next time, you will once again witness madness."

That story offers these four lessons: 1) The entire planet is groaning with pain and suffering caused by our inhumanity. 2) The solution _is not_ isolation and withdrawal having as little contact with the world as possible. 3) The solution _is_ meditation-- quiet time spent listening and accessing our deepest humanity _and_ divinity. _It is meditation which helps us self-heal and self-correct._ 4) Finally, meditation should lead us to be more deeply engaged with life and more committed to transcending our inhumanity. As more people follow this path in life, transcending ourselves from our inhumanity becomes more probable.

LIFE

APPRECIATING _YOUR_ HUMAN LIFE

> If we could see the miracle of a single flower clearly,
> our whole life would change.

Today take a moment to think about this Eastern view of a human life. Their view is that the life we have right now is not just a gift and it's not something that just happened. The Eastern understanding is that *you have earned this life.* In the past you have accumulated sufficient good karma to actually be born and have this present life to live.

The Buddha explained this in a couple of ways. Once he was asked by a King to describe we just how rare it is to obtain this human life. The question actually posed by the king was this: "How many human beings from the lower suffering realms will be able to come up to the wonderful human life that you talk about?" To answer the king, the Buddha looked around and saw a large mirror. He picked up a handful of peas and threw them at the mirror. All the peas bounced off. Buddha explained that the chances of getting a precious human life are even less than the change of any peas sticking to the mirror.

Another time the Buddha was teaching disciples and wanted them to understand how precious and rare it is to be alive. He said that if the entire continent became a huge ocean and within that ocean there was a yak yoke floating on the waves and a blind turtle popped up once every hundred years, the chances of obtaining precious human birth would be equip to the chances of that blind turtle emerging with his head poking through the yoke.

Interestingly, the Buddha's observations about the difficulty (or the miracle) of birth is reflected in modern science. Fertility authorities note that it is extremely challenging for one sperm to unite with one egg. They cite the fact that the availability of a hospitable environment for this to happen is rare; that most sperm do not always survive the long journey all the way to the egg especially if there are poor swimmers or if their count is low. That birth takes place is nothing short of a miracle. Add to their scientific view the Eastern perception that you're being here - reading these words - indicates that you, through past actions, have earned the privilege of birth.

Today, take the Buddha's quote cited above and adapt personally: *If you could see the miracle of your birth clearly, your whole life would change.* Now ask yourself these kinds of questions: "How does this affect the way I live, work, and treat others?" "How does this affect my attitude and life goals?"

LIGHT

TRY TURNING ON THE LIGHT

> Be a lamp to yourself.
> Work out your liberation with diligence.
> **Buddha**

Awakened by thirst, a woman got out of bed heading to the kitchen for water. While walking through the dark house she bumped into a chair scraping and bruising her right shin. Because of the pain in the right leg, she hopped through the room on her left leg. A few seconds later, she banged into another chair, scraping the other leg and tearing her nightgown. In tears, she filled the air with angry cries. Limping further along, she tripped over a small footstool landing on her side bruising several ribs.

By now she wasn't only frustrated but very, very angry. Her blood pressure rose as did her rage. Sitting down on a chair she lamented to herself: "Why am I so clumsy?" "How is it that accidents seem to follow me everywhere?" As she sat there feeling negative about herself, another voice inside her – this one kinder and gentler - responded: "Why don't you turn the light on?" All that was necessary for her to avoid self-injury was to turn on the light.

Her experience is a metaphor about the way many people live. They feel as though they are groping about in the dark. In the process they experience self-inflicted injuries. Rather than continue to live unskillfully, the corrective lies in simply turning on the light.

Perhaps you know people who seem to flow from one disappointment to another, from one error to another, from one misstep to another, from one disastrous relationship to another. Groping about in the darkness makes no sense when light is available. The Buddha reminds us that we have a light within - "Be a lamp to yourself. Work out your liberation with diligence." We simply need to turn on the light thereby reducing self-inflicted pain while permitting spiritual growth and evolution to take place.

LOVE--A LESSON IN COMPASSION FROM EMINGWAY

> Wherever there is a human being, there
> is an opportunity for kindness.
> **Seneca**

One of Ernest Hemingway's short stories is titled *The Capitol of The World*. In it the Nobel prize-winning author tells about a father and his teenage son, Paco. Their relationship deteriorates. Paco runs away from home. The father, distraught, begins a long journey searching for Paco. Unable to find him and as a last resort, the father puts an add in the city newspaper of Madrid. It reads: "Dear Paco, meet me in front of the newspaper office tomorrow at noon...all is forgiven...I love you." The next morning in front of the newspaper office were eight hundred men named Paco

That story is filled with insights worthy of further consideration. First it shows how easily estrangement can be ended. It just takes one side to reach out with the healing and welcoming words "all is forgiven...I love you." Secondly, the large number of men named Paco who showed up to receive love and forgiveness is staggering. There were eight hundred of them. That points out the huge number of people on the planet who feel estranged and want reconciliation. Thirdly – and perhaps most importantly - the story reveals perfectly this basic Buddhist teaching: we are all interconnected, wanting the same thing from life: to be loved and accepted. The father knows this and understands he has the power to offer to his son.

Is it possible that Hemingway, via this short story, was reminding all of us that we can be like the father, that we have it in our power to offer what people need - love and acceptance.

M

MEDITATION

MEDITATION: RELAXING BODY AND MIND

> *Meditation is an innate opportunity to return to a more relaxed state of mind and take a moment to quiet down*
> **David Simon**, MD

A young man, curious about meditation and wanting to derive some of its many benefits, approached a Zen master with this question: "What is the first step for a successful meditation practice?" The Zen master, sensing the young man learned best via visuals, picked up a stick and wrote in the dust on the ground the Japanese symbol meaning *attention.* "But surely there must be more to it than that?" the student objected. Again the master picked up the stick and wrote *attention.* "But what else? There must be more to it," the student pleaded. A third time the master took up the stick and wrote on the ground *attention, attention, attention.*

Many studies demonstrate that meditation delivers enormous benefits - physical, mental, emotional and spiritual well being. Meditation is not an esoteric, complex, mysterious activity. The Zen master is quite right: all that is required is attention or concentration to focus and still the mind. Whenever we can still the mind - even for a few seconds - we are entering into meditation.

Here is a simple meditative technique called 'CPR' because it revolves around the words *clam, peace, relaxed.* It is specifically used to still and focus the mind as well as calm and sooth frayed emotions. Find a place where you can be alone. Sit comfortably with your spine erect. Take two or three deep breaths. Then continue the breathing pattern and recite repeatedly these three statements:

> I am *calm.*
> I am at *peace.*
> I am *relaxed.*

Simply doing this for a few minutes can restore a sense of peace and tranquility in your life. You can practice this mediation in many places and many ways. It can be done while waiting for a bus, subway, at an airport. You can also use it in the privacy of your home and even at your place of work. Just remember to pay *attention.* Repeat the three statements attentively and in a focused, intentional way. That will keep your mind from randomly wandering all over the place.

MENTALITY

WHAT'S THE STATE OF YOUR MIND

> *Without the discipline of guarding the mind,*
> *what use are any other disciplines?*
> **Nagarjuna**

Pause right now and ask yourself, *what kind of mind do I have?* There are many possible answers. Consider....
We can have a peaceful mind.
We can have an angry mind.
We can have a calming mind.
We can have a stressful mind.
We can have a compassionate mind
We can have an untamed mind.
We can have a joyful mind.
We can have a stubborn mind.
We can have an insightful mind.

We can have an arrogant mind.
We can have a humble mind.
We can have a self-defeating mind.
We can have a self-affirming mind.
We can have a wild mind.

The truth is that the mind can be unpredictable and undisciplined, sometimes acting like a trickster in our lives. Normally, we think of the mind as something reliable - and it can be - but there are times when the mind seems to be playing with us. A friend of mine was on a lengthy bike ride across rural Oklahoma with her husband. Each wore a bright orange polyester backpack filled with snacks and water. Her husband was in the lead because he knew the roads. Suddenly on a deserted country road, a black and white medium sized dog came running out of the front yard barking threateningly. The dog did not see my friend's husband but noticed her and began chasing after her. The creature continued the chase coming closer and closer to her ankles.

She certainly didn't want to deal with a dog bite so she pedaled faster and faster trying to get away. Terrified, she didn't dare to look back for fear the slight hesitation would allow the dog to reach her legs. So, she kept driving her legs harder and harder, faster and faster. "I could hear the dog running just behind me. He wasn't barking anymore, but I could hear him panting," she recalls. Her hands gripped the handle bars, knuckles white with fear. Pedaling even harder, she was moving quickly and covering a considerable distance. By now, her legs began to ache and she was having difficulty breathing enough air to maintain this frantic pace for escape. She couldn't understand how a dog could keep up for such a distance. Exhausted, she looked over her shoulder to see if the dog was beginning to tire and slow down. When she turned, she was surprised *and* pleased that she couldn't even see the dog. It dawned on her that what she was hearing all the time was not the dog panting and running ever so closely behind but her back pack shifting from side to side while she frantically pedaled. As she slowed down, she wondered how long ago that dog actually gave up on her? The lesson from my friend's experience has to do with the mind. How many times have any of us had a similar experience of thinking something was true, real, and frightening only to examine it more closely and discover that it was none of those things. It was all in the mind. That's why Nargajuna (150-250 CE), an Indian philosopher taught: *Without the discipline of guarding the mind, what use are any other disciplines?* In Eastern teaching, the method to "guard" or train the mind is via meditation. In meditation we slow down the mind, observe our thoughts in a detached way, understand how our mind operates and learn ways it can be re-programmed to serve us more effectively. Meditation is the path to a calm mind, a compassionate mind and ultimately a skillful mind. Here's a simple way to meditate which can be done anytime, anywhere: close your eyes and count your breath from one to ten, then start over. Focus on counting, not thinking. It sounds easy but is quite challenging.

METTA (part 1)

BEFRIENDING OUR SELF

> *You can search throughout the entire universe*
> *for someone who is more deserving of your love*
> *than you are yourself, and that person*
> *will not be found.*
> **The Buddha**

Try this exercise over the course of a morning or afternoon. Simply pause to observe how you talk to yourself and what you think about yourself. Are you frequently critical, judgmental, and intolerant with yourself? Or, are you compassionate, joyful, and grateful with yourself? We are all in touch with an inner voice. For too many people that inner voice if driven by fear, anxiety, anger and ignorance. What more people need is to be connected to our inner sacred voice whereby we befriend our self, speak kindly and gently to our self.

In eastern thought it is readily understood that we are far too hard on ourselves. Buddhism has a solution for this problem and it is called "metta". The term "metta" is comes from the Pali (The language preferred and used by the Buddha) and it means "lovinkindness." Thus sages from the east teach a "metta" practice which is designed to recover the spark of divinity which is within each one of us. The term "metta" comes from Sanskrit term *mitra,* which means "friend." A metta practice, which is more commonly referred to as a loving kindness meditation, simply instructs us to offer blessings to our self rather than cursing and complaining about our self. A traditional Buddhist loving kindness meditation is made up of four short sentences such as:

May I be healthy.
May I be happy.
May I be safe.
May I be free of suffering.

These are to be repeated gently and kindly for our self as a meditation.

May I be healthy. With this meditative prayer sentence we acknowledge our desire to be without physical, mental, emotional and spiritual diseases and injuries.

May I be happy. Even in prime circumstances our minds can make a hell out of heaven. This sentence reminds us that we deserve happiness and joy; that we want to nurture and grow the seeds of happiness which are within us.

May I be safe. Here we express the desire to be safe from danger, to be protected and have places of refuge. We want to be free from accidents, violence, strife.

May I be free of suffering. This prayer meditative sentence is a call for us to access positive energies of freshness and freedom rather than conflict and struggle. It can be spoken even when we have been diagnosed with a life threatening illness where we may be in pain but do not need to experience suffering. This short loving kindness (or metta) meditation should be offered daily for our self.

METTA (part 2)

BEFRIENDING OTHERS

> Be conscious and intentional about
> the wider destiny of others.
> **Victor M. Parachin**

Kabbalah, is a Jewish mystical movement which bears remarkable similarity to Eastern spiritual philosophies. For example, in the sixteenth century, Kabbalistic Rabbi Isaac Luria taught a mystical version of the Big Bang Theory. He said that in the beginning there was pure Being. Pure Being had no manifestations but was the Infinite, Absolute Source of the world. The world as we know it was created as the result of a mystical explosion. The form holding Pure Being, shattered, broke open and scattered the light of God throughout the universe. Those scattered beams of light included countless sparks of divinity which are hidden deep in everyone and everything. That view is strikingly similar to the Eastern viewpoint that the Divine resides in everyone and everything.

Both Kabbalahistic and Eastern teachers go on to explain that the purpose of life is to uncover those sparks of light, repairing and restoring the world to its original purpose and wholeness. This task falls upon those who have already tapped into their inner Divinity. One way to help those around us locate and access the Divine within is to offer the metta or loving kindness meditation for them.

In Buddhist thought, the loving kindness meditation is incomplete when it is only done for ourselves. While eastern teachers unanimously advise beginning the metta meditation with ourselves, they also urge that we extend it like ripples upon the water. After we have repeated the phrases for ourselves several times, we are encouraged to move on and include those near and dear to us. For our family, good friends, partners we offer:

May (name) be healthy.
May (name) be happy.
May (name) be safe.
May (name) be free of suffering.

Continuing to create the ripple effect, we move on from those we know and love to include those who are wounded, hurt and struggling in life. Those who face hardships of any kind are to be recipients of our blessings. These can be people you know and even people you hear about in the news. Include them in the same metta meditation:

May (name) be healthy.
May (name) be happy.
May (name) be safe.
May (name) be free of suffering.

When we are through with this group, we are advised to create yet one more ripple of blessing and that is to offer the loving kindness meditation to those who have hurt and harmed us; those whom we need to forgive. Though this can be difficult, eastern sages challenge us to move in that direction offering the same blessing:

May (name) be healthy.
May (name) be happy.
May (name) be safe.
May (name) be free of suffering.

As you offer metta for yourself, remember to create ripples of blessings and love out toward others on the planet.

MIND
MIND MANAGEMENT

> The disunited mind is far from wise...
> how can it be at peace? When you know
> no peace, how can you know joy?
> **Bhagavad Gita**

While being driven along the India-Pakistan border a bus got stuck in a hole on the road caused by a bomb during a war between the two countries. After trying unsuccessfully to get the bus moving, the driver asked all the passengers to disembark and help by pushing the bus while he revved the engine.

After several minutes the bus had not budged even an inch so the driver got out to re- inspect. What he discovered was that half the passengers were pushing the bus from the front while the other half were pushing from the back.

That story is a useful symbol of the way our minds often

work.

One mind says 'go', while the other says 'stop'.
One mind says 'yes' while the other says 'no'.
One mind says 'proceed' while the other says 'halt'.
One mind says 'it's OK' while the other says "it's not OK'.
One mind says 'go ahead' while the other says 'go back'.
One mind says 'leave' while the other says 'remain'.
One mind says 'speak up" while the others says 'keep silent'.
No wonder we're stressed, confused, lacking in clarity and
life direction. The tool for settling the mind and giving it
focus is meditation. As we sit quietly, the mind's incessant
chatter begins to ease up and we gain the insight we need to
live skillfully and wisely. It is in silence that we can
experience a clear mind which then frees us to be happier and
healthier.

MIND – PART 2
MAKE YOUR MIND YOUR ALLY

Our life is the creation of our mind.
The Buddha as quoted in the Dhammapada

The mind is very, very powerful tool. It can make you sick
and it can make you well. Consider a study done by scientists
at the Baylor College of Medicine on 165 patients with
osteoarthritis of the knee. They had what is commonly called
wear-and-tear arthritis on their knees. They randomly
received one of these three treatments:

> Arthroscopic removal of dead tissue inside the knee
> Arthroscopic washing-out of the knee joint
> placebo "fake" surgery

Arthroscopy surgery involves the insertion of a fiber-optic
device permitting the surgeon to see and do surgical

procedures inside the knee joint. For those who had the placebo treatment, the surgeon simply made a skin incision on the knee to simulate the real surgery. However, there was no insertion of an arthroscope.

Tracking the 165 patients over a 24-month period, researchers assessed the outcomes and were stunned: *the placebo or fake surgery worked as well as those who had the real surgery.* They concluded there was no "clinically meaningful" difference between the three groups. Also, among some who had surgery, their ongoing physical function was worse that those in the placebo group. Though science is now confirming mind power, the understanding that our mind can by our greatest ally or our greatest foe has been taught across the centuries. Some examples include:

Marcus Aurelius - "You have the power over your mind – not outside events. Realize this and you will find strength. James Allen - "You are today where your thoughts have brought you; you will be tomorrow where your thoughts take you."

The Buddha - "Our life is the creation of our mind." The lesson: be careful what you think and how you think. Negativity breeds negativity just as optimism breeds optimism. Make your mind your most powerful ally!

MIND – PART 3

ELEPHANTS AND TAMING THE MIND

> Rule your mind or it will rule you.
> **Horace**

Elephants have been domesticated by humans for centuries.

Mahouts, who train elephants found that they could never train the trunk which was forever questing in search of interesting things to smell or eat. This became a problem during religious processions because the elephant is marched by pilgrims walking toward a temple. Often the route involves passing along narrow streets lined on both sides with fruit and vegetable stalls. On more than one occasion, an elephant has been known to grab an entire bunch of bananas off a vendor's stall depositing all of them into his mouth. Eventually, mahouts discovered that the trunk is still when given something to do like holding a bamboo stick or a lotus blossom. Only then will this majestic creature walk, proudly holding and displaying the bamboo stick or lotus in his mouth. No longer does the elephant's trunk wander and grasp anything while on route because now it has something else to hold on to.

An elephant's trunk can be compared to the mind. Unless it has something to hold on to or focus upon, it will wander leaping from one thought to another. The purpose of meditation is to focus the mind. One of the most effective ways of doing this is by giving it something to "hold on to" and that something can be a a sound, a syllable, a word, a phrase or a few sentences which are repeated over and over. Here is an easy-to-do meditation using this technique to tame the mind. Find a comfortable place to sit, either on a chair or meditation cushion on the floor. Gently close your eyes and begin taking deeper inhalations and exhalations. On the inhalation simply say "in" and on the exhalation simply say "out." Do this for three to five minutes at a time.

MINDFULNESS

WATCH YOUR MIND

All that we are is the result of what we have thought.

> The mind is everything. What we think we become.
> **Buddha Siddhartha Gautama**

Here are two true stories which reveal the wisdom of the Buddha's words.

The first one is about a railroad employee who was accidentally locked up in a refrigerated freight car where the temperature hovered around 40 degrees. He shouted and pounded for help but no one heard him. Absolutely terrified, the man left a record of his torment and suffering scribbled on the walls of the freight car. By the time the train arrived at its destination the man had died. Significantly, his death was not due to exposure to freezing temperature but sheer fear. On the day he was locked inside the refrigerated freight car, the refrigeration was not on at all.

The other story took place during a football game in California where several people became ill from food poisoning. The doctor who diagnosed the sick spectators discovered they all drank soft drinks from one particular vending machine so he concluded the sodas inside that machine were contaminated. Hoping to prevent more illness, the doctor conveyed the information to an announcer who in turn alerted, via loudspeakers, the spectators at the game. Shortly after, people who realized they bought sodas from the same machine became sick. They experienced nausea, vomiting; some even felt faint. Ambulances arrived, transporting people to the emergency room of a nearby hospital. It was a scene of much anxiety and confusion. As the situation continued to be analyzed and assessed, the doctor realized the original problem was caused by something else and not the vending machine soft drinks. The people taken to the hospital experienced symptoms, not from poisoning, but from their own mental impressions. As the word spread that the vending machine sodas were not responsible, people reacted initially with disbelief, then bewilderment, then acceptance and finally experienced complete recovery. Their symptoms soon disappeared and they walked out of the emergency room.

These two incidents dramatically demonstrate the Buddha's understanding that our thoughts have the power to make our lives better or worse. The mind is a powerful tool. Our mind can cause us to be creative or cruel; to inspire or to injure; to heal or to hurt. The perceptions we form and the thoughts we have can bless ourselves and others or they can harm ourselves and those around us. Choose your thoughts carefully. Watch your mind. Learn to think skillfully so that you are the master of your mind and mastered by your mind.

MINFULNESS (part 2)

MAKING DECISIONS MINDFULLY

> *When you listen, listen;*
> *when you eat, eat;*
> *when you walk, walk;*
> *when you drive, drive.*
> **Victor M. Parachin**

One of the famous ancient Greek stories is that of Midas who was king over ancient Phrygia (today's country of Turkey). Because of his kind and gentle spirit, Midas was noticed by the God Dionysus who wanted to reward him for his good deeds by granting Midas one wish. Without thinking deeply, King Midas asked Dionysus to make everything he touched turn to gold. When his wish was granted, King Midas tested it by touching a tree. Immediately it turned to gold. The king touched a horse and it became solid gold. Everything touched by King Midas turned to gold: Quickly he was becoming the richest human being in the world.

However, major problems began to emerge. When he was hungry and sat down to eat, the food he touched turned to gold as did the wine he tried to drink. Because his simple wish was granted anything he touched turned into solid gold: his water, his bed, his clothes, his friends, and eventually the whole palace was gold. Worst of all, when his daughter came and hugged him, she was turned into gold. Realizing his request was a huge blunder he pleaded with Dionysius to take away his golden power. Dionysius instructed King Midas to bath in the Pactolus River. Taking his golden daughter, he went to the river as instructed and bathed. Both of them were change to their previous state.

The common interpretation of this Greek myth is the warning against greed and amassing wealth as one's life goal. However, that negative interpretation is not the one which is reflected in modern times. Whenever the name 'Midas' is invoked, it is done so in a positive way. Often when someone is identified as a great financial success, that person is described glowingly as "having the Midas touch."

Perhaps a more appropriate way of interpreting this myth is to understand it is a teaching about mindful decision making. When Midas was told he would receive one wish, he rushed into it blindly, mindlessly, without a trained mind which would absorb all of the implications connected to his wish, "Let everything I touch turn into gold."

Today is a good time to look at your decision making process. Do you make them mindfully or mindlessly? What has been the result of some important decisions you made recently? Were they wise or disastrous? Did they produce the results you hoped for or did they complicate and frustrate you? The best way to avoid costly errors in judgment and decision making is to be mindful. This means paying attention, being aware, and being fully present when decisions need to be made. A good way to train yourself to be mindful is to apply it daily to all the routine tasks of your life - from what you wear to what you eat; from how drive to how you listen to others. Be mindful with every action and activity. *When you listen, listen; when you eat, eat; when you walk, walk; when you drive, drive.*

MINDFULNESS – PART 3

LEARNING TO PAY ATTENTION

> Life is available only in the present moment.
> **Thich Nhat Hanh**

Too often we're not really paying attention. Consequently, we miss out on many of life's delights and pleasures. The antidote to this is to simply pay attention, moment by moment and – as the story below reveals – even mouthful by mouthful.

A prominent chef and food writer was visiting Japan to sample the variety of Japanese cuisine. In one city he was invited to dine at the home of a wealthy Japanese family. His host invited many other guests but informed the food writer he alone would be served a special treat - the blowfish. It is considered a rare delicacy in Japan, partly because the fish is highly poisonous and can be fatal to humans unless it is prepared by a highly skilled chef who carefully removes poisonous elements. If that's not done it becomes a deadly delicacy.

As the dishes arrived, the food writer was eager to sample blowfish and he was not disappointed. The taste was unlike anything he'd ever eaten. When his host asked what he thought of the dining experience, the guest enthusiastically praised the unique flavor of the fish calling it "exquisite". Then, the host explained that the fish he had just eaten was actually a common carp. There had been a mix-up in the plates and another guest was accidentally served the blowfish.

To his credit, the chef/food writer immediately learned an important lesson, namely, that ordinary food can become extraordinary if he paid close attention to each mouthful. The lesson he learned is that of mindfulness, the ability to be completely present and aware of what is happening in the moment. In his case, it was a mouth by mouth moment of awareness which made his ordinary fish taste like that of the extraordinary blowfish.

So, instead of merely letting life pass you by, cultivate the fine art of paying attention. That way you increase your chances of experiencing every moment as a wonderful moment.

MISFORTUNE

REVERSING MISFORTUNE

> When misfortune comes into our life
> treat it as a signal that we will need
> to make an attitude adjustment.
> **Victor M. Parachin**

A woman about to be married said, "I had the hall, the caterer, the clergy and the gown. I just didn't have the groom." Four months before they were to be married, her fiancèe backed out saying "the idea of being married is overwhelming and frightening me."

Of course, the bride was devastated. Invitations were out;

gifts were being purchased; and travel arrangements were being made. She was about to wallow in self-pity when her best friend made a suggestion. Since the bride could not get a refund on the hall, her friend suggested using it as a fund raiser for victims of a recent Asian tsunami.

To her credit, the bride agreed saying "I'll make something good come out of this after all." She found band that would play for free and sold off 160 tickets to friends and family. "I almost didn't mind being there and not being married." For that one evening, she and her friend raised several thousand dollars to help people displaced by the tsunami.

Her experience offers all of us these two invaluable insights. First, we can and must reverse our misfortunes. Let us all take sadness and transform it into gladness. Our own wounds can be healed when we allow our pain to become gain for others. Secondly, a core teaching in Buddhism is that we _must_ adapt ourselves to the way life unfolds and not cling to the way we want or wish it to be. In her case, there was not going to be a wedding or reception so she adapted herself to that reality; she adjusted her attitude. In so doing, her suffering was minimized greatly.

N

NAMAHA

RELINQUISHING CONTROL

> Our real blessings often appear to us in the
> shapes of pains, losses and disappointments;
> but let us have patience, and we soon shall
> see them in their proper figures.
> **Joseph Addison**

This is a Sanskrit word meaning "Not me" or "Not mine" or
"It's out of my hands." It is a reminder that we are not the
ones in control and it is ideally used in meditation for those
times when we experience disappointment because our plans
and hopes are not working out. Here is how to do a
"Namaha" meditation when you're feeling disappointed and
discouraged. Inhale the sentence and exhale on *Namaha* as
you repeat these kinds of statements (you can repeat just one
sentence or a combination of these):

It's not about me. Namaha
All is well. Namaha
There is a greater plan. Namaha
I have faith. Namaha
A way will open. Namaha

As you continue to inhale and exhale, simply keep repeating
Namaha permitting its meaning and faith to penetrate your
consciousness.

One woman, whose three year relationship with her

boyfriend ended abruptly and painfully says: "I wasn't just disappointed; I was devastated. I felt and he felt, we belonged together. Then, one day, out of the blue he told me his feelings changed and it was 'time to move on' with his life." She had started practicing meditation eleven months earlier and remembered the Namaha practice. "Though I was an emotional wreck, I had the good sense to tap into meditation and sat for nearly an hour repeating two sentences: *There is a greater plan. Namaha* and *It's not about me. Namaha.* I felt greatly stabilized emotionally and a little more hopeful about dealing with the pain," she says of the experience.

NATURAL

LESS IS MORE

> *When it comes to spiritual growth and evolution,*
> *less is always more!*
> **Victor M. Parachin**

In the time of the Crusades there was a meeting between the leaders of the European forces and Saladin, commander of the Arab armies. One of the Europeans tried to impress and intimidate Saladin by having one of his soldiers cleave a heavy wooden chair in half with a single down stroke of his broadsword. Using both hands the soldier lifted his heavy sword and, in one stroke downward, split the wooden chair into two halves.

In response, Saladin ordered someone to toss a silk scarf as light and delicate as a spider's web into the air. As it descended, he simply held his scimitar (An Arab sword with a curved blade which broadens as it nears the point) beneath it with the sharp edge upward. When the scarf touched the edge, it sheared in half and fell on either side of the blade without even a whisper as he held it completely still.

Saladin's simple, almost effortless approach made a lasting impression on the European leader. There are times when less is more. That is particularly true of spiritual growth and evolution.

Consider the years Buddha spent in struggle and striving before his enlightenment night. He worked with and tried a variety of extreme practices believing they would lead him to an enlightened state. He meditated, for days at a time on bliss, peace, happiness. When this did not produce the permanent changes he sought, the Buddha shifted his lengthy meditations focusing on spaciousness, consciousness, nothingness and on a state described "neither-perception-nor-non-perception." Though he was able to induce himself into a trance there was still no moment of enlightenment.

Not one to give up easily, the Buddha turned to more austere practices. He stood on one foot in a lake with water up to his neck for days at a time. No difference was detected. The Buddha tired cow practice and dog practice: not speaking, not bathing, not sleeping and vocalizing as if he were a cow or a dog. When nothing worked, he began to reduce his food consumption until gradually he survived on one grain of rice per day. Emaciated, he could touch his belly and feel his spinal column. This did not bring him enlightenment.

Despairing that he would ever achieve enlightenment, the Buddha suddenly remembered a simple natural meditation he learned as a child. He sat under an apple tree at a festival quietly breathing and aware of his breath. Deciding to trust the meditative feeling of his childhood, the Buddha returned to this simple, childlike practice. As he sat under the Bodhi tree, he experienced the state of enlightenment and became awakened. Again, less is more.

As we seek greater spiritual growth, awareness, evolution, we must not do it in such a way that it is a constant struggle and battle. Less is more. The only striving which should take place within us is to be as natural and gentle as possible. We ought to practice a radical simplicity. This is what results in something powerfully profound and life altering.

NATURE

ALLOWING NATURE TO NURTURE

> When I would re-create myself, I seek the darkest wood...I enter (it) as a sacred space.
> There is the strength, the marrow of nature.
> **Henry David Thoreau**

Here is a large lesson from a small child.

Every day after school, the son of a prominent rabbi in their community would come home after school, deposit his back pack in his room and then leave the house through the back door heading into a wooded area behind the house. After several weeks of observing this ritual, the rabbi asked: "Son, I notice that every day you leave our home to spend time in the woods. What is you do out there?"

The son replied: "Father, you don't need to worry. I go into the woods every day to pray. It is in the woods that I can talk to God."
Relieved, the rabbi said: "That's fine but, as the son of a rabbi, you should know that God is the same everywhere."
The son replied with a wisdom beyond his years: "Yes, father, I know that God is the same everywhere. But I am not."

Consider intentionally spending more time alone with nature. This can mean little more than a quiet stroll through a nearby park or a longer stroll along the edge of a lake or river or just sit quietly in your own backyard. Do all you can to periodically get away from the pavement, traffic, vehicles, buildings, people, congestion and noise. Rather than exercise indoors at home or gym, do your exercise outside. Let nature nurture as it did Thoreau: "When I would re-created myself, I seek the darkest wood...I enter (it) as a sacred space. There is the strength, the marrow of nature."

NEGATVITY

PUSHING BACK THE NEGATIVE

> Some run swiftly; some creep painfully;
> all who keep on will reach the goal.
> **Piyadassi Thera**

During the Vietnam War, a village was bombed. Upon learning of the great destruction, Thich Nhat Hanh, a Buddhist monk and teacher sent a group of his students to rebuild the village. As they were near completion, the village was bombed a second time. They started over and then it was bombed a third time. People were ready to give up hope because with each rebuilding, the village was bombed. Yet, Nhat Hanh gave instructions to rebuild. "What is the point of rebuilding a village when it will be bombed again?" he was asked. Nhat Hanh told them if they did not rebuild the village it would mean they had given in to despair.

Most of us are fortunate not to have our community being bombed. However, let's allow that true story to help us in another way. There are times when "bombs" are dropped upon us. They come from others who dismiss our dreams, criticize our actions, reject our goals, judge us harshly. These negative voices can come from family members, friends, colleagues, a neighbor. Such negative words can easily discourage us and dissuade us from moving forward.

At those times, we must follow the advice of Nhat Hanh and continue to keep working, improving, building our lives. If we stop because of another person's negativity we are giving in and giving up. Nhat Hanh offers a powerful lesson: *we must be willing to stand fully in our own shoes and never give up on ourselves.* And, when we are able to do this for ourselves, then we are more able to put ourselves into the shoes of others person and never give up on them. So, push back the negative whenever it's dropped on you.

NIYAMAS

EMBRACING HAPPINESS

> But what is happiness except the simple harmony
> between a man and the life he leads?
> **Albert Camus**

One of India's greatest spiritual teachers was Patanjali. Scholars estimate that Patanjali lived some time between 400 BCE and 200 AD, though they are in disagreement about these dates. He was a spiritual genius whose books on yoga, medicine and linguists are Hindu classics. Among his many contributions to eastern spiritual philosophy are a famous listing of ten commitments. The first five are called "Yamas" and they advise avoiding behaviors which produce suffering. The other five are called "Niyamas" and they advise embracing behaviors which lead to happiness and fulfillment. (Note: Turn to the "y" section to read the Yamas). Here are Patanjali's five Niyamas, five activities which can produce a happy life:

1. *Saucha.* This one is all about clean living. It emphasizes physical, mental, emotional and spiritual cleanliness. We need to keep all clutter out of our lives so that we can live in

a state of calm.

2. *Santosha.* Be content. *Santosha* is understood as leading to the greatest happiness. It is the quality of an underlying joy and balance which cannot be shaken by life's trials and traumas. This was something valued by the Christian St. Paul who wrote: "I have learned to be content whatever the circumstances. I know what it is to be in need, and I know what it is to have plenty. I have learned the secret of being content in any and every situation, whether well fed or hungry, whether living in plenty or in want." (Philippians 4:11-12)

3. *Tapas.* This term means "self-discipline." It also has this related meaning of "internal fire" suggesting that self-discipline generates heat. In turn, the heat burns away impurities and kindles spark of divinity within. It challenges us to exhibit self-determination and spiritual drive.

4. *Svadhaya.* Here the emphasis is upon self-study (inner work) which leads to Self-realization. In Eastern spirituality, self-study is more important than scripture study. Eastern sages understand one can read and study enlightened texts without becoming enlightened.

5. *Ishvara Pranidhana.* This one is all about surrender to a higher power, the Universe of God (or whatever other term you favor). Many people surrender their lives to other life arenas: a job, a profession, a relationship, a hobby. Surrender to the Divine is considered the pinnacle of spiritual practice because it means you are always seeking out the highest goodness in every situation.

Review the five Niyamas from the perspective of your life. Which one(s) do you need to work on right now?

O

OBSTACLES

OBSTACLE OR OPPORTUNITY?

> I have learned silence from the talkative;
> Toleration from the intolerant, and kindness
> from the unkind; yet, strange I am ungrateful
> to those teachers.
> **Kahil Gibran**

Long ago in a small Asian territory ruled a king who saw himself not merely as a ruler but as spiritual teacher as well. Wanting to drive home a lesson, he and some of his aides placed a boulder on a highly traveled pathway. Then, they all hid behind some bushes watching to see if anyone would take the time to remove the boulder. Several of the King's most prominent and wealthy merchants came by simply walking around the boulder. Some of them even complained loudly blaming the King for not keeping the roads clear. However, the complainers made no attempt to remove the boulder. After some time, a person of low rank in the kingdom came along carrying a huge load of vegetables to sell at the market. Upon seeing the boulder, the vendor put down his vegetables trying to move the stone off to the side of the road. After much straining and pushing, he succeeded. As the man bent over to pick up his vegetables, he noticed a purse lying in the road where the boulder had been. That purse contained many gold coins – more than he would ever earn in an entire year – along with a note from the king saying: "This gift of gold is for whomever removes the boulder from the pathway."
That vegetable vendor came into both material and spiritual

wealth. The gold was the material and this lesson was the spiritual wealth he gained: *Every obstacle contains within itself an opportunity.* Think about the "obstacles" in your life. For many of us, our obstacles are other people who are challenging and make our lives difficult. Work to turn those obstacles into opportunities for greater growth and learning. That way a tormentor becomes a teacher. This was the experience of poet Kahil Gibran who says that via obnoxious individuals he learned profound lessons about silence, tolerance, and kindness. The enduring truth which is taught in the story of the vegetable vendor is that burdens can become blessings, that every obstacle has within it a seed of opportunity.

OUTLAWS

IT'S OK IF YOU'RE A SPIRITUAL OUTLAW

> Make an island of yourself,
> make yourself your refuge;
> there is no other refuge.
> Make truth your island,
> make truth your refuge;
> there is no other refuge.
> **Digha Nikaya, 16**

If you're one of those people who has never been able to quite fit into traditional religious beliefs, expressions and structures, you may find company in one branch of the Zen Buddhist tradition. That Zen tradition differs from most other religious traditions in that ritual, worship, doctrine, theology, iconography and scriptures play a minor role and are often disdained. There is, for example, a story about a man who practiced Zen by living alone in a small, frail hut deep in the woods away from everyone. During one brutal and cold winter, the snow would drift into his hut and settle on his shoulders as he meditated. Weary of being cold day after day, the man burned the only piece of wood in his possession. It was carefully and beautifully hand crafted wooden statue of the Buddha, given to him as a gift.

As a result, that man and other Zen practitioners like him have been described as spiritual outlaws, a description they are proud of. Some characteristics of these Zen spiritual outlaws include:

- Embracing insecurity
- Honoring paradox
- Courting the unexpected
- Celebrating the unfamiliar
- Shunning and even ridiculing every orthodoxy
- Volunteering for tasks no one else wants
- Swimming against the tide
- Gladly grabbing the short end of the stick
- Accepting despair
- Disdaining doctrine, dogma, theology
- Neither seeking nor submitting to authority
- Breaking taboos in order to destroy their power
-

As they practice their Zen these ways, they enlarge the capacity of the heart, engage their minds, liberate their spirit, think and live outside of the box. These characteristics are also accurate descriptions of the world's great spiritual teachers: Buddha, Jesus, Muhammad. Their spirits resonate with these words from the Digha Nikaya, a Buddhist scripture sometimes called the "Collection of Long Discourses":

Make an island of yourself, make yourself your refuge; there is no other refuge. Make truth your island, make truth your refuge; there is no other refuge. So, if you're one of those fiercely independent souls whom some view as a spiritual outlaw, you're in good company. It's OK if you're a spiritual outlaw.

P

PATIENCE

LEARNING TO BE PATIENT

> Patient forbearance is the quality which
> enables us to prevent negative thoughts and
> emotions from taking hold of us.
> **The 14th Dalai Lama** (Born 1934)

There was a monk who was very impatient. The more he tried to be patient, the more impatient he became. Consequently, he decided that he must get away altogether, to learn to be patient. So he built himself a little home deep in the woods, far away from any of the villages. Years later, a man was traveling in those woods and met him. The man was amazed to find anyone living alone and so far away from others. He asked the monk why he was there all by himself. The monk explained he was there to learn to be patient. "And how long have you been here by yourself?" the traveler asked. The monk told him he had been there seven years. Stunned, the traveler asked, "If there is no one around to bother you, how will you know when you are patient?" At that point, the monk became irritated with answering questions and shouted: "Get away from me, I have no time for you." We can smile at this story of a monk struggling and failing in his attempt to develop patience. Yet, his story is also our story. More and more evidence reveals that we are people who have lost the virtue of patience.

Consider this incident. Two cars were at an intersection when the light turned green. The man in the first vehicle didn't notice that the light had changed so the woman in the car behind him began pounding on her steering wheel, screaming at the man to "get moving" and directed obscene hand gestures toward him. Still, the man didn't move. Finally, he looked up, saw an orange light and accelerated through the intersection just as the light turned to red. The woman behind him was furious and began screaming in frustration because she missed her turn to get through the intersection. While she was venting, she saw someone approach her vehicle. It was a police officer with his hand on his gun. The officer instructed the woman to turn off her car and keep both hands in sight. She complied. The police officer ordered her to exit car with hands raised.

When she got out, he instructed her to turn around, place her hands behind. Then he handcuffed the woman and frisked her. He took her to the police station where she was fingerprinted, photographed, searched, booked and placed into a cell. After an hour, another officer approached the cell, opened the door and escorted her back to the booking desk. There, the arresting officer was waiting with her personal belongings telling her she was free to leave. He offered this explanation: "I pulled up behind your car while you were blowing your horn, making obscene hand gestures, swearing and shouting at the man in front of you. I noticed the 'Choose Life' license plate holder; the 'What would Jesus do?' bumper sticker; the 'Follow me to Sunday School' bumper sticker; and the chrome plated Christian fish emblem on the trunk. Naturally, I assumed you had stolen the car."

Though that story may be an urban legend it reflects daily reality. Too many men and women are impatient on our highways and streets, resulting in increasing incidents of road rage. Patience is a missing virtue in our culture. Yet, reclaiming patience does not mean having to retreat into isolate at a remote location like the monk cited earlier. Life provides us with ample opportunities to develop patience. Today, life to be your instructor in patience. Let the events of daily life, whether those are large or small, be the source of your education in patience. For example:

- Be patient when you are mistreated.
- Be patient when you don't know why.
- Be patient when you must wait.
- Be patient when you are sick.
- Be patient when you've been gossiped about.
- Be patient when you lose a job.
- Be patient when your children frustrate you.
- Be patient when a friend fails to come through.
- Be patient when someone turns against you.
- Be patient when criticized.
- Be patient when encountering resistance.
- Be patient when job hunting.
- Be patient with step children.
- Be patient with your partner; your family; your friends!

PAUSE

LOOK BEFORE YOU LEAP

> Can you remain unmoving until the
> right action presents itself.
> **Tao** (verse 15)

Our modern proverb, *Look before you leap,* is a reminder for us to think carefully about the possible results or consequences before doing something. Lao Tzu, the Chinese sage credited with writing the Tao says the same thing: *Can you remain unmoving until the right action presents itself.* Behind both sayings is the awareness that for too many people, the first response to an issue is action. The Tao suggest there is an alternative response: inaction. Too often we respond and act out of fear, anger or frustration. Yet, a more skillful response is to simply pause and look before we leap into a response.

A dramatic example of this comes from Qiguang Zhao, a American professor of Chinese. Zhao was born in Beijing. As a teenager, he and his family personally experienced the Cultural Revolution. This was a dark and dangerous period in modern China when hordes of high school and college students – called Red Brigades – were unleashed by Mao Tse Tung to root out people who were not revolutionary enough. Usually this meant those who had higher education or were wealthy.

Because his parents were university professors, they came under suspicion by Red Guards who came to his home search for "bourgeois books and objects". Pounding on the door, they demanded to enter. Zhao's parents opened the door and for nearly two hours, his parents were interrogated and humiliated. The house was also ransacked. Evidently, the Red Guards could not find incriminating evidence so they left. That house search was just the beginning. More groups of Red Guards came in the following few days. Zhao says his parents made a decision which was "probably unique" during the Cultural Revolution. When the Red Guards pounded on the door of their home, his parents would turn off the lights and not answer nor open the door. Group after group of Red Guards came pounding never broke in and simply went away. However, hundreds of thousands were not as fortunate as the Zhao family. During that time many were killed, imprisoned or were exiled into the country where they were forced to do hard, manual labor.

What spared his family was application of the Tao – *Can you remain unmoving until the right action presents itself.* They didn't move. They didn't answer. They didn't open the door. Think about times when someone or some issue comes "knocking at your door." Do you have to answer? *Can you remain unmoving until the right action presents itself?*

PERCEPTION

PERCEPTION BECOMES REALITY

> We are enslaved by anything we do not consciously see
> We are freed by conscious perception.
> **Vernon Howard**

A man who had lived most of his life in a mountainous region of China moved to an area which was primarily flatland. On those plains he built a home with large windows. From any window he could look out and view hundreds of miles of land. When neighbors visited asking, "How do you like the view?" he responded: "The only problem here is there's nothing to see."

Around the same time, another man who had lived most of his life in the flat, plains of China moved to a region which was mountainous. There, he built a home with large windows and from those windows he could look out and see the majestic mountains all around. When neighbors visited asking, "How do you like the view?" he responded: "The only problem with this place is that you can't see anything because all those mountains are in the way."

That interesting contrast prompts this reminder: *who you are determines what you see.* What is all around us does not determine what we see rather, what is within determines what we see. How we view our world and those in it, is usually a direct reflection of ourselves. For example:

- If I am a compassionate person, I will view others as compassionate.
- If I am a dishonest person, I will view others as dishonest.
- If I am a trusting person, I will view others as trustworthy.
- If I am a judgmental person, I will view others as judgmental.
- If I am caring person, I will view others as caring.
- If I am an untruthful person, I will view others as untruthful.
- If I am a sincere person, I will view others as sincere.
-

Perception becomes reality. Our outlook determines outcome. Sometimes when we have a problem with others, the problem may be viewpoint. In that case, it makes more sense to try changing ourselves rather than changing the other person. As we do our own inner work of transformation, we become kinder, gentler, and more compassionate and begin to view others in that same light.

PERSEVERANCE

HOW HIGH IS YOUR PERSEVERANCE LEVEL

> Great works are performed not by strength but by perseverance.
> **Samuel Johnson**

When it comes to spiritual growth and evolution, the women and men who make the greatest progress are those who are most persevering and intentional. The one common quality among those we describe as "spiritual masters" is their intentional perseverance. Consider two individuals separated by centuries. The first one is Dogen (1200-1253) considered the most influential Zen teacher of his era. Though he studied with masters in Japan for 9 years, he was unsatisfied with his progress. Consequently, he made a very lengthy and dangerous journey across the East China Sea and then to inland China in order to study directly with several important Chinese Buddhist teachers. He remained there for five years satisfied he had gained the necessary insights.

At the time, most Japanese Zen practices utilized koans (mental riddles) to startle consciousness into enlightenment. Dogan discovered, however, that simple, silent meditation was a more natural way of experiencing enlightenment. Here is what he said and taught:

> "If you cannot find the truth right where you are, where else do you expect to find it?"

> "Do not follow the ideas of others, but learn to listen to the voice within yourself. Your body and mind will become clear and you will realize the unity of all things."

> "When we discover that the truth is already in us, we are all at once our original selves."

The second person to consider is James Allen (1864-1912), another "spiritual master" whose main quality was his tenacious perseverance. Wanting to develop his spiritual life more completely, one biography notes that Allen "retired from employment" at the age of 38. With his wife and daughter, he moved to a small cottage in the country. There he devoted himself to pursuing a simple life of meditation and contemplation. He died nine years but during that time wrote 19 books and edited "The Light of Reason" magazine. His wisdom continues to influence people world-wide.

Among his many insights are these quotes:

> "For true success ask yourself these four questions: Why? Why not? Why not me? Why not now?

> " You are today where your thoughts have brought you; you will be tomorrow where your thoughts take you."

> "Work joyfully and peacefully, knowing that right thoughts and right efforts will inevitably bring about right results."

These two individuals, one ancient and one closer to our times offer this lesson: real spiritual growth and evolution is more likely to take place when our practice is daily rather than sporadic: when we are intentional, disciplined and persevering. And this, of course, is true in any successful life endeavor.

POTENTIAL

BE ALL THAT YOU CAN BE!

> Life's natural tendency is toward the flowering of potential, toward limitless advance. And faith is the key to that enables us to open up to the full realm of possibilities within our lives.
> **Daisaku Ikdeda**

Today, read and reflect on the above sentences from Buddhist educator and philosopher, Daisaku Ikdeda. Look at them carefully:

"Life's natural tendency is toward the flowering of potential."

"Life's natural tendency is toward....limitless advance."

His observation is certainly true in the natural world. Take, for example, a tree. No tree says to itself . . ."I think I'll just grow to four feet and stop" . . . "I think I'll just grow out 2 branches; that will be good enough for me" . . . "I think I'll grow out just 3 leaves; that's enough."

On the contrary, a tree will grow to be as tall as it can possible become. It will grow branch after branch, leaf after leaf. An apple tree never decides, "I think I'll just produce five apples. That's good enough for me." On the contrary, an apple tree will produce as many apples as it's capable of. In fact, an apple tree can produce such an abundance that the weight of the apples can cause its own branch to break. Yet, we human beings are not like the tree. On this planet, only human beings choose to limit themselves. At some point they quit developing, quit learning, quit growing, quit evolving. And, we do this not because we are forced or to have to but simply because we make the choice.

So, ponder carefully Daisaku Ikeda's wisdom: *Life's natural tendency is toward the flowering of potential, toward limitless advance.* That statement is as true for us as human beings as it is for trees. We need to be like the tree becoming as large, expansive, and productive as is our potential. Ikeda wisely adds that what it takes for that to happen is faith....

.... faith in ourselves;
.... faith in our ability to overcome;
.... faith in our inner wisdom;
.... faith in our inner strength;
.... faith that the universe is a place of abundance not scarcity.

Live up to your potential. Be all that you can be!

PRANAYAMA

THE POWER OF PROPER BREATHING

> For breath is life, and if you breathe well
> you will live long on earth.
> **Sanskrit Proverb**

Pranayama comes from the Sanskrit language and is made up of two words: *prana,* meaning life force or vital energy of breath and *ayama,* meaning to lengthen or extend. Thus, in Eastern thought (especially in yoga) *pranayama* is regulating one's breathing in order to bring more oxygen to the blood and to the brain, and to control the vital life energy called *prana.*

Most Westerners tend to ignore breathing because it's so automatic. However, when we are stressed, our breathing tends to be fast and shallow. In those cases, we use of only a fraction of our lungs and the result is a lack of adequate oxygen. This can lead to different complications such as fatigue, stress, heart disease, sleep disorder. By practicing deep and systematic breathing through Pranayama, we reenergize our body. Consider this simple story.

A man attended a week long arts and music festival in Nevada. Called Burning Man, it is an annual event which draws more than 50,000 people. Strategically placed at the festival is an old fashioned phone booth with a sign reading "Talk to God." People at the festival are invited to pick up the phone and talk to "God". God's voice at the other end would listen and then help the caller experience relief from pain or wisdom for dealing with life.

The man spotted this odd sight, went to the phone booth and

called "God". The voice came on the line asking: "How may I help you." The man replied that he was stressed by life's pressures and asked: "How can I live more in the present moment?" He explained that too often he felt the meaningful and beautiful moments of his life were overlooked because of his anxiety and stress. "What can I do to help myself?"

"Breathe," was "God's" reply. The man flinched at something so simple and something which sounded far too new age for him. However, "God" added: "Whenever you feel anxious just breathe. Try it with me a few times right now. Breathe in....breathe out." The man complied and despite his doubts he could begin to feel himself relax.

, consider following "God's" advice the next time you are stressed. Pause and breathe in breathe out. In fact, you can improve your mental and physical condition by simply practicing this pranayama exercise several times a day.

PRESENT

ARE YOU REALLY, REALLY PRESENT?

> When walking, walk! When eating, eat!
> **Zen Wisdom**

Eastern teachers often say that most people are unaware of how much they miss in life because they don't pay attention. Though they are present, they really aren't there. Here's one example. A devotee was traveling on a train with his guru. On the ride he mentioned to his guru that after several years of meditation and studying sacred texts he had not yet had a spiritual experience. The guru then asked him to describe the train conductor who had just taken their tickets. "Was he younger or older? Was he tall or short? Was he heavy or thin?"

The devotee admitted he didn't notice the conductor at all even though he handed him his train ticket. The guru said: "That's why you are missing spiritual experiences." The many sights, tastes, smells, sensations of daily life are missed simply because we're not _really_ present. We listen but don't hear. We look but don't see.

Here's another example done by psychologists Daniel Simons and Daniel Levin. They conducted an experiment to determine how much people were aware of what was going on right in front of their eyes on the campus of Cornell University. They recruited a person to carry a campus map and ask unsuspecting pedestrians if they could give directions to a nearby building. As the directions were being offered, the psychologists had also arranged for two people to walk between the questioner and the pedestrian while carrying a large door. For a a few seconds the pedestrian and the questioner were hidden from each other by the door. During those few seconds, a second questioner replaced the first one. The pedestrian being asked for directions remained the same. So, when the door passed by, there was a different person standing there – different clothing, different height, different size, different hair.

The purpose of the experiment was to determine how many people being asked for directions would notice the change. As it turned out, _not many._ In the first experiment only 47% and in the second round only 33% noticed that there had been a change. Think about that, especially the 2nd time the experiment was done – two thirds of the people were not aware that something had happened right before their eyes. That's why Zen teachers advise: "When walking, walk. When eating, eat." Too many people sleepwalk through life unaware and oblivious of what's really going on. They are not in the present moment taking. Their minds are actually elsewhere. This is how life slips away from us – little by little and moment by moment. When it all adds up, we can miss out on our lives.

PRIORITIES

PRIORITIZING WHAT'S IMPORTANT

Action expresses priorities
Gandhi

Long before he became in influential teacher of meditation, Eknath Easwaran (1910-1999) had the same problem with meditation that most people do: making time for it. Though he began to see the wisdom and benefit of meditation and wanted to do it daily, he couldn't see how to fit it in. "I had an extremely busy schedule, with responsibilities from early morning until late at night," he says in his book *Take Your Time.*

After struggling with his calendar he made the commitment to make meditation a top priority. So, he made a list of all the things he felt he was obligated to do. Then he took out a red pencil and began crossing out everything which was not actually necessary or beneficial. The list surprised him. "I found I had been involved in activities that I couldn't honestly say benefited anyone, including myself. I had simply become used to doing them." Initially his red pencil exercise seemed painful but Easwaran quickly discovered it became liberating as he freed up a number of hours every week. His meditation practice became a daily reality. Additionally, he discovered that several of his activities were actually expendable.

Why not consider doing what he did. Make a list of everything you feel you must do. Then, take out a pencil and cross out activities which are optional and not essential.

Perhaps like Easwaran, you will find you have more time to do things which are important to you – more time for your partner; more time for your family; more time for a beloved pet; more time for meditation; more time to help another person; more time for friends. It all comes down to simple priorities!

PROBLEMS

PROBLEMS AS COMPLIMENTS

> You may not realize it when it happens, but a kick in the teeth may be the best thing in the world for you.
> **Walt Disney**

The next time you face a serious problem (and by that I mean anything and everything from a divorce, death, illness, or just a very difficult person in your life) try looking at it from this Buddhist perspective. In Buddhist thought a huge problem is thought of as a compliment. The problem is a sign you are ready for it; that you are an 'old' soul, enlightened, wise and mature. The problem would not come to you if the universe did not believe in you and your ability to deal with it. Furthermore, the problem is also a a test or life exam to see if you are ready to rise to the next level of enlightenment.

Here's an enviable example of someone who "received" a problem in just this Buddhist spirit. Cynthia was employed by a power plant in Oregon when she and the other 1,500 employees learned the plant was shutting down. Of course, that mean their jobs were ending. For Cynthia this was now an additional burden added the two she was already dealing with. Her mother was dying of brain cancer and her marriage of nearly 3 decades was ending in a divorce.

Naturally, she became worried but at the same time was able to remain both dispassionate about this and be very much in the present moment. This allowed her mind to be a little more focused and, as the layoffs began, she noted high level anxiety about finances among her co-workers. So she volunteered to write a column for the employee newsletter on ways to save. Called "Saving With Cynthia," the column was a hit as it covered everything from buying less expensive car insurance to making pantyhose last longer. That column and her upbeat attitude made an impression on managers of her parent company, Portland General Electric. The very day she received her layoff notice, they hired her in a new position at a higher salary. "If it weren't for the layoff, none of this would have happened. It opened up a new world for me," she says. But, of course, it was her wisdom and maturity which opened up that new world for her.

Whatever the problem you are facing, you can handle it! The problem with problems is that too often we don't handle them skillfully. When you face an issue, pause, take a deep breath and say to yourself "I can handle this!" or "I will find a way to handle this!"

Q

QUAGMIRE

HOW STUCK ARE YOU?

> We have to learn ... to be free of attachment
> to the good experiences and free of aversion
> to the negative ones.
> **Sogyal Rinpoche**

An eastern parable tells about a type of trap set to capture a monkey. The basic ingredient is a type of sticky substance similar to tar. To make the trap, some of this sticky tar is spread on a path known to be used by monkeys. Before long a monkey comes along and steps in the sticky tar. At first only one foot is stuck. In trying to free itself, the monkey puts down the other foot only to discover it too is stuck. Then, it puts down one hand which is also stuck. Next, it places down the other hand. Finally, in a desperate attempt to generate some leverage and gain freedom, the monkey puts its head down. Now five body parts are quite stuck, trapped, frozen in place.

This parable applies also to we humans who often end up in a similar quagmire or entrapping position. For many people the real question is not "Are you stuck?" but "How stuck are you?" The things which entrap us are always mental: desire, attachment, anger, fear, envy, comparing, judging, demeaning etc. It can be quite a long list. Those mentalities keep us stuck and trapped making us very unhappy.

The way for us to remain free is by not walking on that

emotional and mental pathway which trap us. Only when we can do that we will not find ourselves in a quagmire, trapped by our own doing.

QUANTULATE

MEDITATION AND "CRITICAL MASS"

> Ignorance and weakness draw destruction.
> Awareness and enlightenment enlarge compassion.
> **Victor M. Parachin**

Quantulate is a mathematical and scientific term meaning "to calculate the magnitude of" something. This word can be connected to meditation. In the early 1970s, Maharishi Mahesh Yogi (who had an undergraduate degree in physics) taught the value of having a "critical mass" of people practicing group meditation. He even attached a number saying that if 1 percent of a population of 10,000 would meditate in a group, there would be a discernible reduction of violence in the community and that positive, cooperative behaviors would be enhanced.

His view was put to the test in 1981 at the height of the Civil War in Lebanon. A Lebanese medical doctor living in a village of just over 12,000 people in the Chouf mountains, began teaching meditation. Eventually, he persuaded 1 percent or 120 people to meditate regularly as a group. Shortly after the 1 percent began meditating, the violence stopped in that village. Though the level of violence resulting from the civil war continued to rage all around, the village with 120 meditators was spared.

Another person who put Maharishi's claims to a test was Dr. John Davies who conducted an experiment in the small Australian town where he was pursuing a master's degree. He noted that "crime dropped once one percent of the population was meditating."

The theory behind this has something to do with the built-up energy of group consciousness. When many bodies, minds, hearts, spirits are aligned, focused and integrated, there are positive benefits.. We actually experience something of this energy when we walk into a meeting and can "feel" the anxiety, anger and hostility emanating from the group. Similarly, we've had the experience of walking into a meeting experiencing warmth, friendliness and ease. It seems that when we meditate in a group, energy is amplified and reaches a "critical mass" which changes the environment. It seems that meditation may not be as passive as it appears.

QUESTIONS

TEN QUESTIONS TO ASK YOURSELF

> He who knows other is wise;
> He who knows himself is enlightened.
> **Lao Tzu**

In Eastern spiritual philosophy, self-knowledge is a highly prized objective. Here ten questions to ask ... *and answer* for yourself. The sooner, the better.

1. Since death is certain but the time of death is uncertain, what is the most important thing for me to know or do?
2. When was the last time I did something for the first time?
3. Who do I love and what am I doing about it?
4. Would I be friends with myself?
5. What is the best use of each day of my life?
6. What am I doing to help others?
7. When I to go to bed at night and look back at the day, am I satisfied?

8. Am I experiencing joy; am I bringing joy?

9. If those who know me best gave me one piece of advice, what would they say to me?

10. What would I like people to say about me at my funeral?

R

RELIGION

WHAT'S THE BEST KIND OF RELIGION?

> Let your religion be less of a theory and
> more of a love affair.
> **G.K. Chesterton**

The 'best' kind of religion isn't one which has a label –
Christian, Buddhist, Hindu, Muslim, etc., it's one which
stresses the virtues of love, kindness and compassion. Here
are three people who offer their wisdom about the 'best' kind
of religion.

The first is from Larry Winget, a writer from Texas:

"Find a religion that ask only that you LOVE YOUR
FELLOW MAN (his upper case emphasis). Find one that
causes you to stop judging others and teaches you to help
others. When you do, I bet it won't have the words "First" or
"Southern" in its name."

The second is from the Dalai Lama:

"This is my simple religion. There is no need for complicated
philosophies not even for temples. Our own brain, our own
heart is our temple. The philosophy is kindness."

The third is from poet Ella Wheeler Wilcox: "So many gods,
so many creeds, so many paths that wind and wind while just
the art of being kind is all the sad world needs."

Though these three are quite different personalities, they each agree on the 'best' kind of religion – one which has as its core approach the virtues of love, kindness and compassion.

RESPECT

SHOWING RESPECT TO ALL

> A man should wander about treating all creatures
> as he himself would be treated.
> **Sutrakritanga** 1.11.33 (Jain Scripture)

Ikkyu (1394-1481) was a highly revered and influential Japanese Buddhist monk. A poet and beggar, he is credited as one creator of the famous Japanese tea ceremony. One Zen story tells about wealthy, powerful citizens who invited Ikkyu to a banquet where he was to be the guest of honor. Ikkyu arrived but was dressed in his beggar's clothing. The host, not recognizing him, chased him off the property and into the streets. Ikkyu returned home, changed into his ceremonial robe of purple and returned. This time he was received with great respect and ushered as an honored guest into the banquet room. There, he put his robe on the cushion saying: "I believe you invited the robe since you showed me away a little while ago." Then he left. The lesson: don't simply focus on those who are important and powerful, but treat everyone you encounter with profound respect. Treat everyone the way you would want to be treated. This concept is so important that it appears, in a various form, among all the great religions of the world. For example:

Jainism: "In happiness and suffering, in joy and grief, we should regard all creatures as we regard our own self." Lord Mahavira, 24th Tirthankara

Baha'i: "Blessed is he who prefereth his brother before himself." Baha' 'U' 'llah Tablets, 71

Buddhism: "Hurt not others in ways that you yourself would find hurtful." Udana-Varga 5:18

Christianity: "Do for others what you want them to do for you." Matthew 7:12

Confucianism: "Do not unto others what you would not have them do unto you." Analects 15:23

Hinduism: "This is the sum of duty: do naught unto others which would cause you pain if done to you." Mahabbarata 5:1517

Islam: "No one of you is a believer until he desires for his brother that which he desire for himself." Sunnah

Judaism: "What is hateful to you; do not to your fellow man. This is the law: all the rest is commentary." Talmud, Shabbat 31a

Native American: "Respect for all life is the foundation." The Great Law of Peace

Sikhism: "Don't create enmity with anyone as God is within everyone." Guru Arjan Devji 259, Guru Granth Sahib

Zoroastrianism: "That nature only is good when it shall not do unto another whatever is not good for its own self." Dadistan 'i-Dinik, 94:5

Having read these, work at putting this spiritual principle into daily practice: treat everyone you meet the way you would like to be treated.

RESPONSE

RESPONDING VERSUS REACTING

> There are profit and loss, slander and honor,
> praise and blame, pain and pleasure in this world
> the Enlightened One is not controlled by these
> external things; they will cease as quickly as
> they come.
> **Buddha**

In the early 20th century, mystic and spiritual teacher George Gurdjieff, had a school near Paris which attracted spiritual seekers from all over Europe and North America. There, Gurdjieff employed a handyman who was not easy to get along with. In fact, students were irritated by him and frequently complained about him to Gurdjieff.

One day a group of them played a joke on the handyman which so upset him that he quit his job. When Gurdjieff learned what had happened, he went to considerable effort to track the man down, offer apologies and plead with him to return offering an increase in pay. He agreed.

Then, Gurdjieff called all the students together for a meeting in which he announced the handyman had returned to work. The students publicly expressed disappointment. However, Gurdjieff explained the man's value was far beyond his work as a grounds keeper and handyman. Gurdjieff told them the man was, in fact, their best teacher because he irritated them and thus forced them to see if they could skillfully manage their frustration and anger. Even the Buddha noted that we will always be surrounded by people who push our buttons. We'll all experience, via others, "loss, slander, blame and pain." Those who are skillful – or, as the Buddha put it, "the Enlightened" will find ways of responding not reacting to irritating and frustrating individuals. The way we learn that lesson is by viewing such individuals as teachers sent our way to help us develop patience and insight.

REVIEW

REVIEW THE SWEET SPOTS OF YOUR LIFE

> Give thanks for everything in your world that
> cooperates to give you life and strength.
> **Ignatius Loyola**

Here is a universal truth: *no one needs to be taught to have
negative thoughts!* These seem to come naturally, easily,
instinctively. Positive thoughts, however, require attention,
effort and discipline. That's why spiritual teachers across all
religions stress the importance of thankfulness. Above is a
quote from the Christian mystic Ignatius Loyola. The Dalai
Lama makes the same point: "Everyday, think as you wake
up, today I am fortunate to be alive, I have a precious human
life."

Here's a simple way to maximize your gratitude quotient.
This exercise is particularly useful when you are going
through a tough time. Instead of feeling self-pity, instead of
feeling depressed, instead of feeling angry, challenge yourself
to list one hundred blessings in your life.

Though this may seem like an impossible task, just go ahead
and being your list writing positive things randomly. Don't
pause to edit yourself, just write them down as they come to
mind. One man did this, citing 100 blessings. Here is how his
list began:

- Being alive
- Good health
- Having a job

- Comfortable condo
- Friendships
- Reliable vehicle
- Computer
- Internet access
- Clothing
- Free time
- Two cats
- Sleep...

His final entry was "that I have 100 blessings to be thankful for." So, the next time you face a discouraging and daunting challenge, review the sweet spots of your life by listing one hundred blessings which are present.

RYOKAN

SIMPLYFYING LIFE

> If you want to find meaning, stop
> chasing after so many things.
> **Ryokan.**

Ryokan (1758-1831) a Japanese Zen poet lived most of his life as a solitary hermit. He can be an attractive figure for those who are frustrated with the world which seems to get more complex and contentious. As a young man he renounced to train as a Buddhist monk refusing to accept support even from his family. Though it was not required, Ryokan committed to absolute poverty begging daily for his food. Even then, he hated to waste food and what he could not consume, he would place into a pot. Over time, the food would spoil and become infested with maggots. When warned on the dangers of eating it, he replied: "No, it's fine. I let the maggots escape before I eat it and the food is good."

Ever humble, he refused to be acknowledged by any titles including that of priest or poet. There was also an admirable compassion about Ryokan which extended to everyone he encountered. One evening, a thief entered his hut at the base of a mountain only to discover there was nothing to steal. Ryokan returned and saw him there saying: "How unfortunate you have come all this way to my hut and find nothing. Please take my clothing so you do not leave empty handed." Bewildered, the thief took the clothing from a naked Ryokan and quickly left. It is doubtful if that thief could ever forget his encounter with Ryokan. After he left, Ryokan sat outside naked watching a beautiful full moon and is reported to have said: "Poor fellow. I wish I could have given him this beautiful moon." That last comment may be an interpretation of this poem by Ryokan:

> The thief
> *Left it behind-*
> *The moon at the window.*

Along with the beautiful poems he left behind, it is Ryokan's detached and carefree life which appeals to people today. He seldom heard or read news and seemed oblivious to world affairs. Committed to simplicity, the writing of poetry and playing with village children – all to the scorn and ridicule from others – he nevertheless left his mark. One of his most popular poems reflects his philosophy and his wisdom:

My hut lies in the middle of a dense forest:
Every year the green ivy grows longer,
No news of the affairs of men
The sun shines and I mend my robe.
When the moon comes out, I read Buddhist poems
If you want to find the meaning, stop chasing after so many things.

S

SAMENESS

WALK IN SOMEONE ELSE'S SHOES

> Strive at first to meditate upon the
> sameness of yourself and others.
> **Shantideva** Way of the Bodhisattva 90:8

Here is what's behind Shantideva's words (he was an eight
century Indian Buddhist monk): is the truth that too many
people focus upon differences between people. A smaller
group puts their focus on similarity between people.
We create a false identity when we view ourselves as
different from others. It simply results in a false sense of self
and security. As a corrective to this propensity of seeing
ourselves as different – usually meaning superior and better
than other – Shantideva wisely suggest we focus or meditate
upon "sameness of yourself and others." To do that try
walking in someone else's shoes. Try to connect their life
experiences with your life experiences. What is common
among us is far greater than what is different. Here is a
powerful example of what can happen when we follow
Shantideva's advice to "meditate upon the sameness of
yourself and others."

Buddhist teacher Jack Kornfield tells the story of a group of
musical Tibetan monks, famous for their deep multi-vocal
chanting, who were to perform in California's infamous San
Quentin Prison. That would be followed by a performance
from the San Quentin Prison Gospel Choir. As the date
approached, organizers became concerned there would be a

cultural and religious gap between the two groups. The members of the gospel choir were all African Americans. While in prison, they had come to embrace Christianity exhibiting the enthusiasm common to new converts. Organizers were concerned that these new Christians would view the Tibetan Buddhist Monks as foreigners practicing a false religion. They wanted to find a way to bridge this gap and overcome all differences. One of organizers came up with an inspired solution to the dilemma by introducing them this way to San Quentin prisoners.

"Almost all of these Tibetan men who have joined us today have spent years in harsh prisons. The Communist Chinese Army not only imprisoned them for expressing their beliefs, but tortured them as well. Somehow they were released or able to escape from prison. Then, to find freedom, they walked across the Himalayas, the highest mountains on earth. Some tied rags on their fee because they had not good shoes. But even now from their families and community, they do not know if they will ever be able to return. What has kept them going through all of their struggle have been their songs and prayers. This is what they will sing for you today."

The prison energy was instantly transformed with that introduction. The Tibetan Monks chanted as the African American gospel choir listened intently. When the gospel choir took its turn singing, the Tibetan monks were equally mesmerized. Both groups sang from a common heart and from a common life experience. When it was over, African American men and Tibetan Buddhist monks hugged and embraced each other like long, lost brothers.

Today, walk in someone else's shoes. Try to see what is similar and the same between you and that person. Put into action, Shantideva's wisdom: *Strive at first to meditate upon the sameness of yourself and others.*

SELF

ELIMINATING BOUDNARIES

> No self, no other.
> **Zen Saying**

A North American spent time in India's Old Delhi. His heart was pierced when he came across entire multigenerational families living on a single patch of sidewalk which they claimed as their own. Though he placed money in their hands, he left feeling this made almost no difference and was crushed by the impotence of his charity. Returning home, he mentioned the incident to a spiritual teacher he respected highly.

Interestingly, his teacher had witnessed the very same types of people in Delhi. Acknowledging that such sights hurt the heart, he went on to say that the poor on the planet should not simply be regarded with pity. Rather, our eyes and hearts must be open enough to see what they have to teach us. Citing the family living on a single patch of sidewalk, he said they are people who take care of each other every single day while living as an extended family. Though they are poor, they practice values which many of us have lost sight of he reminded his friend.

I had a similar learning moment, but this one in my own community. There are several homeless men who frequent a busy intersection which I jog by. Since I see them regularly, we have become friends. One day I stopped to give one of the homeless men a few dollars. As we visited, he told me that a few days earlier at the same intersection, he placed his bike behind him and turned away as he held up a sign saying "I need help." As he was soliciting money, a pickup truck stopped behind him. Two men leapt out, grabbed his bike, put into the truck and sped off. I told him how badly I felt this happened. However, he surprised me by smiling and saying: "You know, I just decided to laugh about it and nothing else. Otherwise the alternative was to be angry and bitter. The bike just wasn't worth that!" I've reflected on his wisdom many times.

While we should always help the poor, our acts of charity and compassion ought to be infused with gratitude for what they teach and offer us. Our view of the poor, the homeless, the struggling single parents, must have a boomerang effect. We see their condition *and* we learn invaluable lessons from them. Life is a unity. There is no outsider, no insider. *No self, no other.* We are all for one and one for all.

SELF – PART 2

WHO ARE YOU REALLY?

> You too can be a Buddha, an awakened
> being that lives and responds in a wise,
> creative, and compassionate way.
> **Martine Batchelor**

In ancient Tibet there lived a farmer who had a few acres of land. One day he learned that a monk was reportedly living in a cave on the mountain adjacent to his farm. The farmer had great respect for such monks and great admiration for their spiritual practices. Thus, he decided to observe the monk. So he made his way to the monk's cave and quietly sat some distance away. In the shadows or a rock overhand, the farmer saw the monk deep in meditation. He noted that the only items the monk seemed to own were a cooking pot, a sleeping mat and a small bag of flour. The farmer's respect and admiration deepened.

From then on, the farmer began bringing milk, yogurt and flour to the monk in order to help support him. Some months later, the farmer thought "perhaps the monk will offer me a spiritual teaching if I ask." So, the next time he dropped off his supplies, he asked the monk to offer him a simple lesson which would help him spiritually.

Instead, the monk suggested that the farmer make a pilgrimage to a nearby lake. "There you will have a vision. No lesson I could offer you would be better than the vision you will experience there." When the farmer asked "how long must I stay at the lake before I see the vision?" the monk said: "Only one day. You will see the vision the same day you arrive."

With considerable excitement and enthusiasm, the farmer made his way to the lake. There, he sat by the lake's edge and stared into the deep blue waters. He waited, waited and waited some more. He saw nothing except some floating leaves, some stones below the water and some reflections. The farmer was deeply disappointed and returned home. The next day he climbed up the mountain reporting to the monk that his pilgrimage was a failure. There was no vision. "I saw absolutely nothing," he told the monk.

"Nothing?" asked the monk.
"Nothing but some leaves, some stones – and, oh, my reflection."
"Ah, then you did see the Buddha. You saw the Buddha perfectly."

The next time you feel discouraged, disappointed, perhaps even despairing about your life, look into a mirror – any mirror will do: in the bathroom, in the bedroom, a car mirror, a make-up mirror – You will see the Buddha. Who are you really? Your real nature, your true self is that of the Buddha.

SELF - PART 3

HONORING THE SELF

> A vital life skill lies in knowing
> when it's time to move on.
> **Victor M. Parachin**

It's a good mental exercise to remind ourselves occasionally that we cannot be everything to everyone. There are limits to what we can, who we can work with and how much success we can have with others. Those limits need to be honored and respected. Doing so is a sign of healthy self-esteem.

Even the Buddha faced limits. In fact, one of his titles – an odd one at that – was *The Teacher of Those Who Can Be Taught.* As history shows, the Buddha was a highly effective teacher but *not all the time.* At one Buddhist monastery there was great discord and a complete lack of harmony. There the monks bickered and fought with each constantly. One group accused the others of not following the rules. The accused denied it charging the other group violated monastic rules by making false accusations.

When the Buddha learned of these difficulties at the monastery, he personally visited offering these recommendations:

- that the monks apologize to each other for misunderstandings
- that they refrain from complaining and

criticizing
- that they work diligently to maintain harmony

After many discussions them, it became clear to the Buddha that they were not open, nor agreeable to any of his suggestions. So, he thanked them for their hospitality and left content that he had tried to help even though it was to no avail.

Through that incident the Buddha offers this important lesson about honoring the self. Rather than cling to the mistaken idea that we can be everything to everyone in every situation, we must bring compassion to bear upon ourselves recognizing and respecting our limits. Like the Buddha, we need to limit our perfectionist impulses.

SENTIENT

HONORING *ALL* BEINGS.

> When a man has pity on all living creatures,
> then only, is he noble.
> **Buddha Siddhartha Gautama**

"Walk a mile in his shoes" is a contemporary proverb. The idea behind that wisdom saying is that we experience deeper empathy and compassion if we try to feel another person's pain. That concept is recognized and valued in Eastern thought as well. However, Eastern sages push it to a broader level challenging humans to extend the same compassion to *all* sentient beings including animals. The story is told of a man named Wu Yang.

Wu and his son spent a lot of time in the forests. They weren't there to enjoy the scenery but for hunting. Wu was a highly skilled marksman with his bow and arrow. He seldom missed. His hand and eye coordination were superior. Wu was such a good shot he barely took time to aim. No animal was quick enough or agile enough escape his arrow. One day he and his son spotted a fawn. Wu whipped an arrow out of the quiver and immediately the fawn fell over dead. Then Wu noticed its mother a few feet away in the grass. He couldn't get the shot he needed from his angle so he waited. When the mother saw her dead fawn, she let out a wail and began licking the fawn's bloody wound. As she concentrated on her fawn, Wu let off another arrow killing the mother deer on the spot. Wu now heard another sound in the tall grasses. Even though he had already killed two deer, he thought to himself "Three deer are better than two."

So, he sat quietly waiting for the third one. Hearing a sound and seeing the grasses rustle with movement Wu fired an arrow directly into the area. Proudly he heard another body collapse to the ground. His pride turned to anguish and horror when he approached the body only to see that he had killed, not another deer, but his own son who had been hunting with him. He heard a voice deep within himself saying: "Wu Tang! Now you know what it is like to see your baby shot to death with an arrow. Animals love their young as much as you do. Consider how much anguish you have caused animal mothers and fathers." Wu stood there numb and heartbroken and never hunted again.

Eastern sages tell that story because they want us to learn this lesson: All sentient beings - creatures which experience sensation and feelings - want the same things: happiness, safety, security. The Buddha reminds us that we must honor _all_ beings - *When a man has pity on all living creatures, then only, is he noble.*

SHAPE

YOU ARE RESPONSIBLE FOR SHAPING *YOUR* LIFE

> As an irrigator guides water to the fields,
> as an archer aims an arrow,
> as a carpenter carves wood,
> the wise shape their lives.
> **Buddha**

A woman tells of "hitting a new low" in her life. She was broke, newly single and overweight. Often she lamented to her friends about her overdrawn bank account, her bad dates and her increasing weight. Before long her friends grew weary of her endless personal dramas. One friend, however, recommended she attend a motivational workshop.

Believing she had nothing to lose, the woman registered. On the first day, the leader asked everyone to share stories about times they felt victimized by life. This was, of course, an easy assignment for her so she told tale after tale of being rejected by employers, banks and men.

After permitting everyone to share, the speaker then asked them to make a mental shift: "What if you were accountable for what happened. How did *you* end up in those situations?" he asked them to consider.

Initially, the woman resented any inference that she was somehow to blame for the fact she was single, in debt, over weight and generally going nowhere with her life. Reluctantly, she took on the challenge of thinking about herself and the choices she'd made in the past. She recalled buying a new pair of shoes when her rent was due. She remembered eating a chocolate dessert when she was on a diet. She reflected on the distance she created between herself and the men who asked her out on dates because she wanted to cover up her vulnerability. And, she recalled ignoring the red flags as she pressured her now ex-spouse into marriage. As she reviewed and re-told these stories in this new way, she experienced relief not regret.

Ultimately, by accepting responsibility for the state of her life she gained the power to shape her future. Rather than feeling like a victim, she began to be an advocate for her life realizing she had the power to live differently. Not surprisingly, over the next twenty-four months she found satisfying employment, lost weight and is dating a "wonderful" man.

This is exactly what the Buddha had in mind when he offered this teaching:

> *As an irrigator guides water to the fields,*
> *as an archer aims an arrow,*
> *as a carpenter carves wood,*
> *the wise shape their lives.*

The majestic quality we have as human beings lies in our ability to remake ourselves. Just because our past has been dark does not mean that our future will be dim. No matter what our past has been, no matter what our present reality may be, the future is pregnant with unlimited possibilities because we are the architects of our lives. It is up to us to shape, fashion, and design our living.

SILENCE

HEALING POWER OF SILENCE

> The most profound statements are often
> made in silence.
> **Victor M. Parachin**

A popular proverb states "silence is golden." A better version could be "silence is noble." Just as skillful speech is important, so is skillful silence. A counselor tells of facilitating a weekly self-help group. One of the rules was that no one commented on anything said by another member during the sharing time. They were not even permitted to say, "I agree with you" or "A friend went through a similar difficulty." The members were there for one reason only: to listen.

One evening a young woman came. When it was her turn to speak she explained her 37 year-old husband had recently died from cancer. As she spoke, there were moments when she could not be understood because of heavy crying. To hear a person pour our such pain and be unable to respond felt strange and awkward to the members. Yet, they followed the rule of only listening and not commenting in any way. The young woman came for several weeks and then reported she quit attending her other support groups saying "I'm receiving exactly what I need from this one."

Upon hearing her words, the members realized the healing power of silence. By allowing her to express and experience her pain without judging or offering a pious platitude, she was able to find her own way. At the same time, the young woman found herself in the company of people who were fully present to her and held her in silent compassion. It was all very powerful and very therapeutic for her.

SILENCE (part 2)

LISTENING TO SILENCE

> Stop talking and thinking, then there
> nowhere you cannot go. Returning to

the source, you gain the meaning; chasing
forms, you lose the wholeness. A moment's
true insight transcends all.
Sosan (died 606)

Indira Gandhi, former Prime Minister of India, often
consulted with a spiritual teacher (Dhirendra Brahmachari)
whenever there was intense turmoil during her
administration. On one such visit, she was accompanied by a
journalist friend. Flying by private plane to her teacher's
ashram, Ms. Gandhi was taken immediately to be with him
alone. After a few hours she returned to the plane. She and
her journalist companion returned home to New Delhi. The
journalist reported that a deep sense of serenity and peace
seemed to have come over the Prime Minister. So, the
journalist asked: "You appear more relaxed, less tense. What
happened in your meeting?" Her answer caught the journalist
by surprise: "It was wonderful," she said. "I put all my
questions to him and he answered every one of them, but
neither one of us spoke a word."

Here is one way to understand Ms. Gandhi's experience. The
insightful power of silence, exhibited so strongly by her
teacher, awakened a similar remembrance of her own. She
was reminded that in quietness an understanding can emerge
wherein vexing questions are either answered or simply fade
away.

While this may seem esoteric and rare, anyone can tap in this
same intuitive wisdom which comes out of silence. The next
time you are tormented by a troubling issue try some of these
techniques:

- Turn the sound off. When you're in your car or
  even in your home, keep things quiet - no YV,

no radio, no CD, nothing!
- Go for a long walk, run or bike ride (again, no headphones).
- Let nature help you. Drive yourself to a forest, large park, or lake. Meditatively walk with nature.
- Meditate. Even if you've never meditated before, find a place in your dwelling when no one else is around and simply sit quietly.

As you engage in these kinds of silent activities, let your mind become still like clear water and allow fresh insights to emerge. Just listen to the silence, that still small voice within each one of. Then, the inner wisdom will make itself known.

SIMPLICITY

JUST DO IT!

> I expect to pass through this world but once;
> any good thing therefore that I can do, or any kindness
> that I can show to any fellow creature, let me do it now;
> let me not defer or neglect it,
> for I shall not pass this way again
> **Stephen Grellet**

In ancient China, there lived a monk who liked to meditate at the same time every day perched high up in a tree. Weather conditions never deterred the monk from his daily meditation time. Sunny and warm or rainy and cold, the monk was there sitting high in the tree every when it swayed in fierce winds. Because of this unusual habit, he was nicknamed "Birdnest" by the local villagers. Many of them passed beneath the monk while hunting or gathering wood in the forest. Sensing his friendliness and openness, they would stop and share their concerns with Birdnest. His gentle suggestions and insights were appreciated by all. Before long he had a well earned reputation for wisdom.

Over the years the monk's reputation spread from the village to the entire province and visitors from distant cities hiked to the remote forest seeking out his counsel. One day the governor of the province - an older man - decided to visit Birdnest to gain insight. So, one spring morning he set off to find him. After a journey of several days he found the monk in a dense forest sitting calmly high in the topmost branches meditating and enjoying the spring warmth and the singing of birds. Looking up, the governor shouted: "Birdnest! I am the governor of this province and I have come a great distance to speak with you. I have a most important question." The governor waited for a response but heard only the pleasant sounds of leaves moving in the breeze. So he continued: "This is my question Birdenest: can you sum up what all the wise ones have taught?" There was a long pause - only the movement of the leaves and branches were heard.

Finally, the monk shouted down from the tree. "This is your answer governor. *Don't do bad things. Always do good things.*" The governor was irritated. He felt this answer was far too simple to have walked several days for. Clearly annoyed, the governor mimicked the monk: "*Don't do bad things. Always do good things.* I knew that when I was three years old, monk!" Looking down at the governor, Birdnest responded courageously and honestly: "Yes, the three-year-old knows it; but the eighty-year-old still finds it very difficult to do!"

The observation of Birdnest is accurate. There is an endless shortage of people who actively try to do good. That may have been in the mind of writer Stephen Grellet who said: "I expect to pass through this world but once; any good thing therefore that I can do, or any kindness that I can show to any fellow creature, let me do it now; let me not defer or neglect it, for I shall not pass this way again." You know that kindness and goodness are important. Put them into practice today and tomorrow and tomorrow again. Life does not need to be so complex. It can be as simple as "just do it!"

SKILLFULLNESS

MANAGING DRAMA AND TRAUMA SKILLFULLY

> When love and skill work together, expect a masterpiece.
> **John Ruskin**

The Lotus Sutra is possibly the most important scripture to Buddhists in the Mahayana tradition. It is the form of Buddhism practiced in China, Vietnam, Korea, Tibet, and Japan. The Lotus Sutra is important because it is believed to contain the Buddha's final teachings.

In it, a story is told about the burning house. The owner, who has been away, return to find parts of it engulfed in flames. He can hear his children playing inside, oblivious to the danger. At first, he screams for them to flee the house and come outside. However, they ignore his cries because, not seeing any fire themselves, prefer to keep on playing. Call after call fails so the father tries another approach. He calls out to them joyfully announcing the he has come home and brought special toys for them to play with. There is a new and different toy for each child. Excited by the prospect of new toys, the children all run outside and are saved from the flames.

Of course, this is an unusual story and its oddity is what gives it instructive power. It is a story about us and there are two important lessons for us to learn from it.

1. Are we like the father who acts skillfully to help his children escape danger? This story invites us to look at ourselves and assess our skill level when it comes to dealing with others. Do we respond skillfully or react in ways that are unskillful? Whenever our approach lacks skill, we are unsuccessful. But, when we find creative, positive ways to approach others, the results are beneficial.

2. Are we like the children who are preoccupied in an activity that we are unable or unwilling to hear concerns and warnings from others?

This story is about our acting skillfully in life. It is about right thinking, right speaking, right acting when the various dramas and traumas of life come our way.

SPIRITUALITY

COMMITTING TO BEING ON A SPIRITUAL PATH

> Look and you will find it - what is unsought
> will go undetected.
> **Sophocles**

A man engaged the Buddha in a conversation about spiritual practice. The man told the Buddha he could not begin such a practice until many of his philosophical questions and life issues had been resolved. In response, the Buddha said: "It is as if a man had been wounded by a poisoned arrow and when attended to by a physician were to say: 'I will not allow you to remove this arrow until I have learned the caste, the age, the occupation, the birth place, and the motivation of the person who wounded me.' That man would die before having learned all this." The Buddha went on to explain the same principal applies to individuals who will not commit to living a spiritual life _until_ they have resolved all of their concerns, questions, and issues about spirituality. Buddha would say, "Such a person will die before all such matters are properly understood and decided."

Here is the important lesson the Buddha was trying to teach the man: *a spiritual life does not begin at the end.* It does not start after we have resolved all differences and contradictions. We must begin at the beginning. Spirituality is like a seed. Locked within it is tremendous potential for growth, awareness, maturity, enlargement and enlightenment. Yet, that seed is useless until we plough, turn, fertilize the soil and follow-up by planting, watering, weeding, and nurturing that seed helping it emerge and blossom.

The Buddha's wisdom is as applicable today as it was in his day. Currently, many people hesitate making the commitment to be on a spiritual path. They believe they have ample reasons to hold off and hold back: *I have too many questions. I don't have time. I'm not ready. I'm sick. I'm handicapped. I'm an alcoholic. I'm addicted. I'm in prison. I've been burned by toxic religion. I'm struggling in my relationship. I'm unhappy at work. I'm too busy, etc.*

If you're one of these people, the Buddha would say: "For your own peace of mind and life happiness, you can enjoy the benefits of living a spiritual life without having to get your life in order nor having a complete understanding of all the profound underlying theories." The Buddha would advise you to simply make the commitment to live a spiritual life now. Put yourself on the path today. Don't allow your issues and questions to block your spiritual growth and evolution. *Remember the ideal time to begin a spiritual practice is always now.*

T

TAOTAOIST QUESTIONS TO PONDER

> When I let go of what I am,
> I become what I might be.
> **Lao Tzu**

Lao Tzu was a Chinese philosopher who lived sometime in
the 4 century BCE. He reacted to and satirized the prevailing
Confucian thought of the day. In a culture which was
dominated by Confucianism - it was the popular and
prevailing world view - Lao Tzu was a refreshing and
unconventional voice. He often asked questions which others
never thought of. Here are some samples of Taoist inspired
questions for you to ponder:

*When you have nothing to do, can you let yourself do
nothing?*

*Are you able to prevent leisure and guilt from holding hands?
Must action always be the first response to an issue or an
injustice?*

*Is it possible to drown with information but be starved for
wisdom?*

Can you see the opportunity in an unfavorable condition?

Are you courageous enough not to care what others think?

Do you walk in the rain or do you just get wet?

Can you take a break from your mind?

Are you wise enough to be lenient to yourself and lenient to others?

Can you correct, change and live without regrets?
Is it possible for you to walk without a destination, goal or objective?

Does every problem need fixing?

Can you see that not everything that looks wrong is broken?

TEACHERS

BEING AWARE OF TEACHERS

> You have the Buddha-nature. But without the help
> of a teacher you'll never know it.
> **Bodhidharma**

A well established, centuries old monastery was made up of just men from its beginning. Everything changed when a beautiful young woman came to the abbot requesting to be admitted to the monastery. She made her case saying she had been meditating several hours daily, studying various sacred texts for several hours daily and now wanted to be part of a community dedicated to the same spiritual ideals.

Though hesitant, the abbot was much impressed by the young woman's commitment and devotion so he said "yes, you may join us." It took the monks time to adjust to having a woman present and most of them were accepting. However, some secretly fell in love with her. One of them wrote her a letter telling her that he was madly in love with her and asked that she met him at a certain time in a specific location. That evening as the community sat for meditation, the young woman stood up and said: "To the monk who wrote me that letter - if you love me as much as you profess, come forward now and show me."

This story probably never happened but it is cited by Eastern spiritual teachers for the purposes of developing deeper insight. It raises two questions: 1) how should the story end, conclude? 2) what is its meaning?

Consider the first question about concluding this story. I shared this with a meditation group asking how they would complete the story. One smiling woman said "It would be a wonderful end if all the monks stood up declaring their love for her!" While that's an interesting possibility here is another. If the monk really loved her, he should have the courage of his convictions and declare his love openly, not keep it hidden. However, if he continued to keep his feelings secret, he might have been guilty of confusing love with lust. Lust thrives in the darkness or secrecy but may not survive the scrutiny of light and openness. If he didn't come forward, the woman would rightly suspect he wasn't really in love with her.

Now, consider the second question: what is the meaning of this story. Uncovering that we need to look more closely at the man who wrote the love letter. By going public, the woman provided him with an opportunity to recognize his lust and come forward admitting it. By her action she gave him a chance to confront an undesirable aspect of himself. The question we can ask ourselves: Who are the individuals who come into our lives providing us challenging opportunities to confront and deal with our dark side, that part of us which we find undesirable and in need of corrective action. Rather than resent them, we ought recognize them as teachers, be grateful to them and acknowledge the opportunity for growth which they provide us. Perhaps we can even learn to be thankful for everyone in our lives who is a problem. Bodhidharma, the Indian monk who came to China in 520 and founded the Ch'an (Zen) sect of Buddhism, wisely reminds: "You have the Buddha nature. But without the help of a teacher, you'll never know it."

THINGS

SEEING THE SPIRIT IN THINGS

> We may even derive right instructions from nature, from trees and flowers, from stones and rivers.
> **Piyadassi Thera**

In Native American tradition as in all indigenous cultures there is a concrete belief that everything has a "spirit" - trees, flowers, stones, rivers, lakes, etc. Furthermore, the spirit in those 'things' is a source of respect and learning.
However, in our culture, too often we take for granted 'things' around us. To offset that tendency, here's an exercise for you to try sometime for just a few minutes. Think of a 'thing' which you use frequently – perhaps, your automobile, your cell phone, your computer, a book. Then, offer a gratitude meditation for that 'thing' listing the many ways it has been good to you. One man, viewing an old battered chair which he took when it was abandoned in an alley, citing these benefits which have come to him via that chair:
- It was free and came to him when he was a poor college student, so impoverished he didn't have the money to buy a chair at a thrift shop;
- It supported him through a senior thesis, a master's thesis, a doctoral dissertation, and three versions of a book he was writing;

- It allowed him to sit comfortably reading hundreds of professional reports, magazines and books;
- It held him as he cried, laughed and rocked his babies to sleep.
- It has never required a repair, never frustrated him in any way.

His experience is what indigenous people identify as the 'spirit in things'. They are to be respected, appreciated and learned from. Removing the spirit from 'things' is partially to blame for our current environmental crisis. Hindu author Swami B. V. Tripurari notes:

" Our present environmental crisis is in essence a spiritual crisis. We need only to look back to medieval Europe and the psychic revolution that vaulted Christianity to victory over paganism to find the spirit of the environmental crisis. Inhibitions to the exploitation of nature vanished as the Church took the "spirits" out of the trees, mountains, and seas. Christianity's ghost-busting theology made it possible for man to exploit nature in a mood of indifference to the feelings of natural objects. It made nature man's monopoly. This materialist paradigm has dominated the modern world for last few centuries. The current deplorable environmental crisis demands a spiritual response." One way of responding spiritually to our ecological issues lies in perceiving, recognizing and appreciating the spirit in 'things' all around us.

THOUGHTS

BE CAREFUL WHAT YOU THINK

> Every man takes the limits of his own field of vision for the limits of the world.

Arthur Schopenhauer

When the 20th century Zen master Shunryu Suzuki was asked to sum up the essence of his life philosophy, he replied with in three words: *Not necessarily so.*

Of course, his succinct reply was designed to be a teaching moment for the student who asked. In reflecting on the meaning of his three words, this possibility emerges. Suzuki was reminding us that our perception of what is happening is usually incomplete, lacking in full knowledge and therefore faulty. *We don't see things as they are, we see them as we are.* For example….

…..the anger we perceive in someone else may be arising our of their own wound and hurt;

…..the irritation we perceive in another person may be coming from their own physical and emotional pain;

…..the rudeness we perceive in someone else may have been launched by a bitter experience which took place earlier;

…..the distancing we perceive in a friend or lover may be no more than their preoccupation over an issue pressing on them;

…..the stubbornness we perceive coming from another person may be their cover up of deep insecurity, anxiety and fear;

…..the ill-mannered, rude person we perceive may be carrying a burden no one knows anything about.

When we encounter behavior in others and find ourselves judging (negatively of course), perhaps we could suspend judgment and remember Suzuki's wisdom: *not necessarily so.*

TIME

CHILL OUT AND GIVE IT TIME!

> When in a personal crisis act on this philosophy:
> time will tell.
> **Victor M. Parachin**

Rather than jump to the conclusion that your life is a disaster, or a mess, or impossible, try offsetting those types of thoughts by saying to yourself: *time will tell.* Don't make important or final emotional decisions about your situation while you are in the midst of it. Give it some time. In so doing you will gain wisdom, balance and perspective. As an example, consider these events which took place over a year in the life of one man:

- After working for the same company for 32 years, he was fired at age 53.
- His boss explained the firing by saying "Sometimes you just don't like somebody."
- He was deserted by friends including his best friend who never called after he was fired.
- He started to drink heavily.
- He developed tremors.
- He considered suicide.
- His best job offer was from a company on the edge of bankruptcy.
- He took the job and became widely criticized for the company's worsening problems by the press, the US Congress and many prominent business leaders.
- He gave up his entire salary due to the company's rapidly deteriorating financial condition.
- He began waking up in the middle of the night with panic attacks and fearing that he was going insane.

- He started seeing double.

That man was Lee Iacocca. Five years after being fired he was universally acclaimed for saving the Chrysler corporation and the jobs of its 600,000 employees. His success was so stunning he was widely encouraged to run for president of the United States. Iacocca probably felt the day he was fired was the worst day of his life. In retrospect, that one bad day made everything else possible. The day he was fired may have been the best day of his life.

So, in the middle of a crisis, don't judge yourself. Give it time to evolve and come to a logical conclusion. Life is most impermanent. Nothing ever stays the same for very long.

TOLERANCE

A LESSON IN RELIGIOUS TOLERANCE

> What counts is not creed but conduct. By their fruits ye shall know them and not by their beliefs.
> **Sarvepalli Radhakrishnan**

Hindus of India rightly pride themselves for their gifts to the world. They have given the world yoga. They have given the world meditation. In addition they are models of religious tolerance and acceptance. Historically, the people of India have welcomed, with open arms and hearts, other religious traditions with no thought of changing or converting them. Their attitude is one of complete acceptance of other faiths understanding that all paths lead to the same One, Eternal, Absolute, God. Hindus place their emphasis, not on correct belief, but on search for the Truth, which results in their remarkable and unusual tolerance, something not as readily found in the three major Western world religions - Islam,

Judaism and Christianity. One who has noted, with great appreciation, this Hindu generosity toward other religious traditions is Dr. Nathan Katz, a university professor and an authority on Jews in India. Here are his glowing comments about Hinduism:

"Jews have lived freely in India for perhaps two thousand years. Hindus pride themselves on tolerance, and India's unique position as the only nation in the world with no anti-Semitism reinforces this cherished self-perception. When Jews come to learn that some of us have lived freely, peacefully and creatively for so long in India, we are surprised and delighted, and we admire Hinduism as the only civilization immune to Jew-hatred. We learn that anti-Semitism is not universal, and that it is possible to preserve Jewish identity and religion in the absence of persecution. For this, we (Jewish people) feel deep gratitude."

Just think how much kinder, gentler and better this planet would be if this kind of spiritual openness and tolerance was present in the lives of more Christians, Jews and Muslims. Here are some inspiring words for all of us who are on a path toward enlightenment. They come from Radhakrishnan, the philosopher President of India (1962-67) in his book, *The Hindu View of Life*. "What counts is not creed but conduct. By their fruits ye shall know them and not by their beliefs. Religion is not correct belief but righteous living. The Hindu view that every method of spiritual growth, every path to the Truth is worthy of reverence has much to commend itself."

TOLERANCE – PART 2

INCREASING OUR TOLERANCE LEVELS

> God is one. Men call Him by various names.
> **Hindu mantra**

Chief Red Jacket (c 1750-1830), a native American who lived in what is today the Rochester, NY area, was an eloquent defender of Native American spirituality. In one of his famous addresses, he challenges white Europeans to practice the religious tolerance. He notes the irony of European presence in America: that they came to escape religious intolerance in their own countries only to become equally intolerant of Native American spirituality. Here is Chief Red Jacket's plea:

Brother . listen to what we say. There was a time when our forefathers owned this great island. Their seats extended from the rising to the setting sun. The Great Spirit had made it for the use of Indians. He had created the buffalo, the deer, and other animals for food. He had made the bear and the beaver. Their skins served us for clothing. He had scattered them over the country, and taught us how to take them. He had caused the earth to produce corn for bread.... If we had some disputes about our hunting ground, they were generally settled without the shedding of much blood. But an evil day came upon us. Your forefathers crossed the great water and landed on this island. Their numbers were small. They found friends and not enemies. They told us they had fled from their own country for fear of wicked men, and had come here to enjoy their religion. They asked for a small seat. We took pity on them, granted their request; and they sat down amongst us. We gave them corn and meat; they gave us poison in return.

The white people, Brother, had now found our country. Tidings were carried back, and more came amongst us. Yet we did not fear them. We took them to be friends. They called us brothers. We believed them, and gave them a larger seat. At length their numbers had greatly increased. They wanted more land; they wanted our country. Our eyes were opened, and our minds became uneasy. Wars took place. Indians were hired to fight against Indians, and many of our people were destroyed. They also brought liquor amongst us. It was strong and powerful, and has slain thousands.

Brother, our seats were once large and yours were small. You have now become a great people, and we have scarcely a place left to spread our blankets. You have got our country, but are not satisfied; you want to force your religion upon us.

Brother, continue to listen. You say that you are sent to instruct us how to worship the Great Spirit agreeably to his mind, and, if we do not take hold of the religion which you white people teach, we shall be unhappy hereafter. You say that you are right and we are lost. How do we know this to be true? We ... only know what you tell us about it. How shall we know when to believe, being so often deceived by the white people?

Brother, you say there is but one way to worship and serve the Great Spirit. If there is but one religion, why do you white people differ so much about it?

Brother, we do not understand these things. We are told that your religion was given to your forefathers, and has been handed down from father to son. We also have a religion, which was given to our forefathers, and has been handed down to us, their children. We worship in that way. It teaches us to be thankful for all the favors we receive; to love each other, and to be united. We never quarrel about religion.

Brother, the Great Spirit has made us all, but he has made a great difference between his white and red children. He has given us different complexions and different customs.... Since he has made so great a difference between us in other things, why may we not conclude that he has given us a different religion?

Brother, we do not wish to destroy your religion, or take it from you. We only want to enjoy our own."

Though Chief Red Jacket's voice on tolerance was not heard in his day, there is increasing awareness of the need for religious tolerance. Too many tensions, hostilities and wars are the result of religious intolerance particularly between Christianity and Islam. The Eastern religions offer humanity the gift of tolerance. There has never been a Hindu war or a Buddhist war. Hinduism, for example, has as one of its guiding teachings this sentence: "God is one. Men call Him by various names." In Hinduism and Buddhism, religious tolerance is the norm. There are no tensions, no need for conversions because there is only one God but many paths. And, each path is respected. The focus is on harmony not difference. Because of this, the Eastern faiths are a lighthouse directing humanity through treacherous religious waters.

Whether you are religious or agnostic, why not practice an increase of tolerance toward those who view religion and spirituality differently than do you?

U

UNRUFFLED

WE DON'T HAVE TO FREAK OUT

> Why not just let the sun shine when it shines,
> why not just let the rain fall when it rains.
> **Zen Proverb**

This Zen proverb is a reminder to work at remaining unruffled, dispassionate, composed and deliberate when things don't go our way. It speaks directly to our tendency to engage in useless worry and abortive battling against events beyond our control.

In feudal Japan, a warrior was captured by his enemies and thrown into prison. That night he was unable to sleep because he feared that the next day he would be interrogated, tortured, and finally executed. As he struggled with those agitating thoughts, the words of his Zen master came to him: "Tomorrow is not real. It is an illusion. The only reality is now." Recalling and heeding those words, the warrior became peaceful and sleep soundly.

That story is one way of understanding the Zen proverb: *Why not just let the sun shine when it shines, why not just let the rain fall when it rains.*

Here is a more current example which comes via a woman whose husband lost his "really good" job. Because this was nothing they ever anticipated happening they made no financial preparations to be without his employment. Their savings were minimal. "We had two choices: freak out, get upset and become so stressed that I couldn't function properly *or* surrender." She and her husband chose not to resist, not to battle, and simply not to worry. "By choosing to surrender and flow with this issue, we both found it to be freeing. We decided to cooperate with wherever life was going to take us and adjust accordingly."

In her case, surrender was not simply giving up and giving in. Rather, it was a deliberate action acknowledging that a Higher Wisdom was operative in their lives. The next time you deal with a painful and stressful issue try recalling and applying this Zen proverb: *Why not just let the sun shine when it shines, why not just let the rain fall when it rains.*

UNSKILLFUL

GOSSIP IS UNSKILLFUL SPEECH

> The temple bell stops but the sound keeps
> coming out of the flowers.
> **Basho**

From the Buddha on, every eastern spiritual teacher cautions against gossip. It is a type of unskillful, unhelpful speech which brings suffering to both the gossiper as well as the target of the gossip. A Jewish Hasidic tale tells of a village filled with remorse for the harm his gossip had caused a neighbor. He visited with his Rabbi where he confessed to his poor deed asking for advice.

Oddly, the rabbi recommended go to the village and buy a chicken bringing it back to the rabbi. On the way home, the rabbi told him to pluck it completely. When the man returned with the featherless bird, the rabbi then instructed the man to retrace his steps and gather every one of the scattered feathers. Astonished, the man replied this would be impossible. By now the feathers were probably blown throughout villages in the area. The rabbi nodded in agreement and the man understood the rabbi's lesson: we can never take back out words. This is one interpretation of Basho's poem (Matsuo *Basho* 1644 – November 28, 1694 was the most famous Japanese Zen master and poet of his time): *The temple bell stops but the sound keeps coming out of the flowers.* Once the bell peals the sound will continue to reverberate.

UNUPSETTABLE

BECOMING UNUPSETTABLE

Develop the mind of equilibrium.
You will always be getting praise and blame,
but do not let either affect the poise of the
mind: follow the calmness...
Nipata Sutta

The Buddha was a human being just like any one of us. He
had problems in relationships and problems with himself.
People knew this about him so they would come to Buddha
with their issues:

"I have problems at home."
"I have problems with my partner."
"I have problems with my children."
"I have problems with my work."

They would complain and lament telling him their problems
displaced all inner-peace and affected their ability to sleep.
To each person who came with a problem, the Buddha had
the same answer. With wisdom and compassion he would
remind them: "Nobody is upsetting you. Nothing is upsetting
you. You get upset because you are up-settable." Of course,
he would not leave them with just that thought. He asked if
they wanted to be "un-up-settable." They always said "yes"
so the Buddha told them: "Then you have to train your
mind."

Most people want to be un-up-settable and be able to respond
skillfully to problems which come their way but many are
simply too lazy to train the mind because it requires focus,
attention, and discipline. Yet, the Buddha and many like him
show us that it's possible to train a mind which remains still,
unaffected by regrets from the past, nor fears of the future.
When the mind is trained to be still or un-up-settable, we
reclaim peace of mind and are able to respond – not react –
the events at hand.

V

VANISH

VANISHING COMPASSION

> Compassion delayed is compassion denied.
> **Victor M. Parachin**

How often has this happened – You see someone in need, perhaps a homeless person begging for money, and have an intuitive, spontaneous impulse to respond. Then that is immediately followed by thinking: *What good will my contribution do for him?* Or *What if the homeless man spends my money to buy liquor or drugs?* Immediately, compassion vanishes. By thinking we override intuition. And in the end, we hesitate. Compassion delayed is always compassion denied. Kindness delayed is always kindness denied. Love delayed is always love denied. This list could go on and on.

That's why the modern Korean Zen Master, Seung Sahn, frequently told his students, "Don't check. Just do!" By that he meant we should immediately respond to our intuitive wisdom rather than allow our thoughts to undermine our original intuition. Whenever a kind or compassionate intention emerges from within us, don't evaluate it, don't analyze it, and don't re-consider it. Instead, trust it. Just do it.

Seung Sahn practiced this approach personally. Sometimes it was dramatic. On one occasion he became concerned about all of the religious division and strife which was tormenting the planet. Intuitively he felt that peace on the planet could be achieved if the prominent religious leaders got together to talk and understand each other – *in a hot tub!* True to his teachings, he didn't evaluate, analyze or reconsider. He didn't check. He just did it. He flew to Rome hoping to convince the Pope to convene just such a meeting *in a hot tub.*

Here's the lesson which we can apply in our own lives: when your wonderful desire to help someone or some organization emerges, don't check, just do it. Just do something! Don't ask yourself: W*hat good will my small contribution make? Should I really be doing this? Is this really a smart thing to do?* Simply trust your inner wisdom. Believe what your feelings are calling you to do and move in that direction. Don't check! Just do it!

VARIETY

VARIETIES OF SPIRITUAL EXPERIENCES

> Everyone is on a spiritual path; most people just don't know it.
> **Marianne Williamson**

Take a moment to re-read and reflect on the above quote from Marianne Williamson: "Everyone is on a spiritual path; most people just don't know it." Think about yourself or perhaps people you know who want to live a spiritual life but are frustrated because they can't find one that works for them. One reason for this dilemma may be due to a constricted view of what a spiritual path looks like. One of the most fascinating aspects of the Hindu philosophy is their development of differing spiritual roads tailored to different human personalities. If you've been frustrated by your religious upbringing or feel limited by it, perhaps you could find your spiritual "place" by locating yourself into one of these spiritual pathways developed by the ancient yogis:

1. *Meditation path*. This one is technically called *raja-yoga* and appeals to individuals who naturally contemplative and need a lot of 'down time'. This person enjoys meditation, alone and with a group.

2. *Exercise path*. This one is technically called *hatha-yoga* and appeals to individuals who need to work their bodies. In a good yoga class, the instructor stresses that the physical and the spiritual goal of yoga is the same: liberation.

3. *Wisdom path*. This one is technically called *jnana-yoga* and appeals to individuals who are intellectually inclined. Their spiritual growth comes from study and application of higher wisdom.

4. *Action path*. This one is technically called *karma-yoga* and appeals to individuals who are passionate about social justice and peace. This path is one of service to humanity and to the Divine. People drawn to this path want to establish the "kingdom of God" here and now for the benefit of all.

5. *Devotional path*. This one is technically called *bhakti-yoga* and appeals to individuals who are drawn to the Divine in a mystical way. These are people who experience a blissful, selfless and overwhelming love of God as a beloved Father, Mother, Child, Friend or whatever other way they relate to the Divine.

6. *Sound path*. This one is technically called *mantra-yoga* and appeals to individuals who are inspired by music. In both Catholic monastic traditions and Hindu temples, chanting is the expression of this spiritual path. In the African American tradition, lively repetitive gospel singing is an important way of experiencing the divine. So, if you're a musician or moved deeply by music, this may be your pathway to spiritual

evolution.

7. *Body path*. This one is technically called *tantra-yoga* and appeals to individuals do 'body work': massage therapists, yoga instructors, personal trainers, fitness workers etc. Unlike most religious traditions in which the body is suspect and even considered "evil" trantra yoga views the body positively and as a powerful tool for connecting with the divine. If you like to work with your body and work with other bodies, this is the path which can awaken and deepen you spiritually.

Interestingly, the Judeo Christian heritage cites four of these paths but lumps them into one single scripture verse: "And you shall love the Lord your God with all your heart (bhakti) and with all your soul (raja) and with all your mind (jnana) and with all your strength (hatha)." (Jesus in Mark 12:30 but he is quoting from the Jewish Bible, Deuteronomy 6:5) The genius of Hindu spirituality is in distinctly living the various paths. Ancient yogis wrote entire books on how to walk each of the spiritual paths.

VILLAIN

SPIRITUAL VILLAINS

> I have always noticed that deeply and truly religious persons are fond of a joke, and I am suspicious of those who aren't.
> **Alfred North Whitehead**

There was a young monk in China who was a very serious practitioner of meditation and spiritual teachings. One day this monk came across something he did not understand, so he went to ask the master. When the master heard the question, he began to laugh and he continued laughing.

Without answering the young monk, the master simply stood up and walked away, still laughing.

The young monk was very disturbed by the master's reaction. For the next three days, the humiliation he felt tormented him. He could not eat, sleep nor think about anything except the master laughing at him. After three days, he went back to the master and told the master how disturbed he had felt. When the master heard this, he said, "Monk, do you know what your problem is? Your problem is that *you are worse than a clown!*" Shocked, the monk said: "Venerable Sir, how can you say such a thing?! How can I be worse than a clown?"

The master explained, "A clown enjoys seeing people laugh. You? You feel disturbed because another person laughed. Tell me, are you not worse than a clown?" When the monk heard this, he began to laugh. He was enlightened.

This story is about spiritual villains. There are people on a spiritual path who take themselves and their journey far too seriously. Not only are they far too serious about themselves, they also expect others to be equally solemn, somber, stern about their own spiritual evolution. They are spiritual villains because they rob others of joy, humor and lightness. The Zen master saw past the monk's question and spotted a spiritual deficiency, something which was an impediment to his growth. Rather than respond to the question, the master laughed and then left the room laughing. This forced the young monk to think more deeply about his spiritual personality. To his credit the monk understood and experienced an important moment of enlightenment. The lesson for all who travel a spiritual path: lighten up and enjoy the journey!

W

WAR

STOPPING WARS ONE MIND AT A TIME

> Wars begin in the minds of men, and, in those
> minds, love and compassion would have built the
> defenses of peace.
> **U. Thant**

Paul Reps (1895-1990, author of the highly popular book *Zen
Flesh, Zen Bones,* studied Buddhism and Haiku all over the
Orient. During the early 1950s Reps wanted to spend time in
Korea studying with a respected Korean Zen master. His trip
meant a stop-over in Japan. There, he went to the passport
office to apply for a visa to enter Korea but was turned down.
The official explained that no visas were being issued
because the Korean War had broken out. Reps was deeply
disappointed as he had planned this trip for months, made all
the necessary preparations to leave his home and had just
traveled thousands of miles.

Not certain exactly what to do next, Reps decided that since
he had unexpected time on his hands, he would meditate
while sipping tea from his thermos. Very mindfully, he
opened his bag pulling out the thermos. Opening it he
watched steam rise from it evaporating into the air. Then he
poured himself a cup of tea. Reps smelled the aroma of the
tea and then began to sip it enjoying both its warmth and
subtle flavor. Finishing his tea, he mindfully put the cup back
on the thermos and then placed the thermos back into the
bag. The combination of tea and meditation produced a

moment of inspiration for Reps. Reaching into his bag, he pulled out a pen and piece of paper. On it he wrote a haiku poem.

Mindfully he walked back to the counter of the visa office, bowed to the clerk on duty and gave him the haiku poem along with his passport. The official read it carefully several times. He smiled at Reps, bowed to him, opened Reps passport and stamped it for entry into Korea. Here's the haiku Reps wrote and presented to the Japanese official:

Drinking a cup of tea,
I stop the war.

Fortunately for Reps, the visa official understood the haiku. Wars begin in the human mind. And, if the human mind can conjure up thoughts of war and conflict it can also generate thoughts of peace and compassion. That's why U. Thant, former secretary general of the United Nations, observed: "Wars begin in the minds of men, and in those minds, love and compassion would have built the defenses of peace." He, along with Reps and many others, believed that wars could be stopped one mind at a time. Written into their constitution is this sentence: *That since wars begin in the minds of men, it is in the minds of men that the defenses of peace must be constructed.*

WISDOM

A LESSON FROM GUTEI'S FINGER

> Believe nothing, no matter where you read it, or who said it, no matter if I have said it, unless it agrees with your own reason and your own common sense.
> **Buddha**

In the ninth century lived a zen master who came to be known as Gutei because he began his meditations by chanting "gutei, gutei". Those syllables began a sentence of his favorite sutra (a sutra is usually a direct teaching of the Buddha). Because he was regarded as a Zen master, people would approach Gutei to ask him about enlightenment. When this happened, the great master Gutei would quietly and simply raise one finger into the air. Gutei would never respond verbally but "answered" by raising one finger.

Before long, a young man in the village began to imitate this behavior. Whenever he heard people discussing Gutei's teachings he would interrupt the sessions and raise his finger. Word of this young man and his behavior reached Gutei who invited the youth to meet with him privately. According to the story, Gutei grabbed the boy's finger and cut it off. Shocked and humiliated, the youth began to run away but Gutei called out to him. When the boy turned to look Gutei raised his finger in to the air. At that moment the young man gained wisdom and enlightenment.

This, of course, sounds like a bizarre story. However it should not be taken literally. While Zen masters could be extremely impatient and even cruel toward their students it is highly unlikely Gutei actually cut off the boy's finger. What probably transpired was a very unpleasant interview between Gutei and the young man which left him feeling as though "Gutei cut my finger off." Setting that issue aside, consider these four lessons this story has for us.

1. **Wisdom or enlightenment cannot be imitated**. Imitation is never a substitute for personal knowledge and wisdom awareness. In Buddhist thought, there is no such thing as gaining wisdom and enlightenment merely by imitation and memorization. There is no concept for a teacher providing a

student with some information which is committed to memory and repeated back on a text earning the student an "A".

2. **Attachment is always counter-productive.** The symbolic cutting off the boy's finger is a reminder that the young man is too "attached" to the teacher and the teacher's style. Gutei actually proves himself to be a Zen master by reminding the boy to detach himself from the teaching. Severing the finger was Gutei's forceful way of impressing upon the youth that it is pointless to copy other people's words and actions without real understanding (in his case, a teacher raises a finger and he blindly follows to raise his finger).

3. **Enlightenment is always individual and personal.** Your enlightenment cannot be mine. Mine cannot be yours. Just as the search is individual and personal, so is the end result.

4. **Blindly following any leader - religious or political - is delusional and dangerous.** Blind obedience and adherence is not the Buddhist way. That is why Buddha always challenged his followers to investigate his teachings by their own and not follow teaching blindly: *Believe nothing, no matter where you read it, or who said it, no matter if I have said it, unless it agrees with your own reason and your own common sense,* is the wise teaching of the Buddha. Because the young man did not understand this profound truth, Gutei severed his finger, held it up for him to see. Only in that moment did the young man understand and become enlightened.

WITHIN

YOU'VE GOT WHAT IT TAKES

Peace comes from within!

Do not seek it without!
Buddha

A distraught man made his way to a Zen center in 13 century Japan. There he was greeted by Zen Master Ikkyu. After listening to man's many difficulties – problems with marriage, problems with work, problems with children etc., Ikkyu responded: "I'd like to offer something to help you but in the Zen school we don't have a single thing." Needless to say, the man was both disappointed and confused.

What was going on with Ikkyu? Was this a lack of compassion on his part? Or, was he trying to convey and important lesson to the man?

His answer wasn't a lack of compassion but it was his way of promoting this important lesson: the answer to our life dilemmas is not outside of us coming from somewhere else or someone else. Here's an example to illustrate that truth.

A friend of mine spent seven years living and studying at an Ashram in India. Periodically Ashram leaders would lead a sacred fire ceremony. The energy of the fire symbolized the energy of the Divine. So, worshippers gather around the fire with an intense upon the Divine placing offerings into the fire while chanting mantras. The fire ceremony lasts many days so my friend's job was to stoke the ashes through the night in order to keep the fire going. Without someone to stoke the ashes, the fire would simply dwindle out because of the suffocating weight of the ashes. Though there were glowing embers buried beneath the top ashes the pit had to be stirred in order for the flame to glow.

Our lives are symbolized by that fire pit. Within each of us is a light. However, the stresses and strains of life are like ashes which cover up and hide the light. Consequently people begin to look outside of themselves for solutions, for happiness, for meaning. Yet, because all of us have that inner light or inner wisdom or the divine within, all we truly need to do is stir the "ashes" of life which have been layered upon us. Meditation is the stirring tool we use to access our inner light and wisdom.

Everything you need for greater health, harmony and happiness is within your reach *because it is within*!

WODEYAR IV, MAHARAJA

USING MONEY FOR THE BENEFIT OF OTHERS

> Money is a beautiful invention, a great blessing
> if rightly used.
> **Osho**

Yoga is extremely popular. In North American millions participate in yoga classes. If you're one of those who appreciates and loves yoga, then offer gratitude to the Maharaja of Mysore, Krishnaraja Wodeyar IV. Without him, yoga may never have left India. Maharaja Wodeyar IV ruled over the state of Mysore from 1902 until his death in 1940. In fact, his family constituted a royal dynasty which ruled Mysor from 1399 until Indian Independence in 1947. Maharaja Wodeyar was so highly regarded that he was often referred as the "saintly king" and the "philosopher King." This was because he used is enormous wealth to support and promote Indian culture. It was the Maharaja who brought T. Krishnamacharya to the palace employing him specifically to popularize the practice of yoga. At that time, the British still ruled India placing an emphasis on European gymnastics and body building exercises. The Maharaja wanted an exercise form which was more culturally appropriate and that was yoga. Also at the time, yoga was not commonly practiced in India and, generally, was limited to Ashrams.

Working under the patronage of the Maharaha, Krishnamacharya was given a wing of the royal palace for offering yoga instruction free of charge to anyone who wanted to learn and practice. His first students were: his son T.K.V Desikachar (Vinigyoa style), his brother-in-law B.K.S Iyengar (Iyengar Yoga Style), his brother-in-law Pattabhi Jois (Ashtanga Yoga Style) and, later, Indra Devi, the 'First Lady of Yoga' in America. Those individuals were part of a yoga dynasty which launched a renaissance of yoga in modern times and one which is still sweeping the world.

So, if you love yoga, offer gratitude to Maharaja Krisnharaja Wodeyar IV of Mysor. And, one more thought: if you are one of those fortunate people who is wealthy, why not consider doing what the Maharaja did: use your money to benefit many others.

WORKPLACE

7 SPIRITUAL DISCIPLINES FOR THE WORKPLACE

> Being aggressive, you can accomplish some things, but with gentleness, you can accomplish all things.
> **Tulku Ugyen Rinpoche**

Many people find their place of work difficult. The challenge of being there for 40 or more hours per week is reflected in the way their workplace is often described:

toxic....dysfunctional....hostile. Since you have to spend so much time at work it makes sense to try and do your part to make the workplace a friendlier, happier and more satisfying place to be. Here are 7 spiritual disciplines to bring into your place of employment:

1. The spiritual discipline of the Golden Rule. The place of work would be more harmonious and people would be more fulfilled if every worker applied the spiritual discipline of the Golden Rule - "Do for others what you want them to do for you." (Matthew 7:12, New International Version) Virtually every major world religion has its own rendition of this principle. For example, Islam teaches: "No one of you is a believer until he desires for his brother that which he desires for himself." Likewise, the Buddha taught: "Hurt not others in ways that you yourself would find hurtful." And Hindus are taught: "This is the sum of duty: Do not unto others which would cause you pain if done to you." Simply paraphrased, all versions of the Golden Rule tells us: "Treat others the way you want to be treated."

2) The spiritual discipline of respect toward all others. Treating other persons in the workplace with fairness and equality is another important spiritual discipline. We must exhibit an honest respect toward all others regardless of their race, religion, color, or ethnic origin. We must view each of our work colleagues as part of a large, extended family.

3) The spiritual discipline of self-respect. Along with the spiritual discipline of respect for others we must also practice self-respect in our work. Buddha said: "Your work is to discover your work and then with all your heart to give yourself to it." Behind Buddha's teaching is the reality that all work is honorable and by working we contribute to the common good.

4) The spiritual discipline of praise and giving thanks. This discipline has been somewhat 'formalized' through special days: Secretaries Day, Bosses Day, Labor Day, birthdays, annual performance review, various anniversaries such as

25th, 30th, 50th etc. However, there are many days in between when others need to be praised and thanked for their contribution. Praise is desirable, pleasing, warming, encouraging, energizing, empowering and reassuring. Humans crave it and thrive on it.

5) The spiritual discipline of listening. Many workers feel invisible. They feel that supervisors, managers, executives don't listen to them when they share ideas and concerns. This is easy to correct: just listen to colleagues and subordinates.

6) The spiritual discipline of serving. In the workplace, the natural tendency to be on the receiving end - receiving a bonus, receiving an attractive salary, receiving a promotion - must be balanced by the spiritual discipline of serving. If someone in your workplace suffering, reach out with compassion. If someone in your workplace has become chronically ill, offer practical aid. If someone in your workplace has been downsized, connect them to other potential job opportunities. If a family member of a work colleague has been diagnosed with a life threatening illness, do whatever you can to ease the heavy load your colleague will be carrying. "A person should be more concerned with spiritual than with material matters, but another person's material welfare is his own spiritual concern," declared Rabbi Israel Salanter (1810-1883) a Jewish leader who emphasized ethical self-improvement.

7) The spiritual discipline of personal integrity. The word 'integrity' simply means honesty and sincerity. Both of those qualities are much needed in today's places of work. Duplicity, hypocrisy, and insincerity among work colleagues is a major source of discouragement and disillusionment in the work place.

WORLD

THE WORLD IS YOUR CLASSROOM

> The world itself has a role to play in our liberation.
> Its very pressures, pains and risks can wake us up-
> release us from the bonds of ego and guide us
> home to our vast, true nature.
> **Joanna Macy**

If you want to soften and even remove frustration and fear, anger and anxiety, depression and despair from your life, then consider this powerful thought: *the world is our classroom.* As we understand that deep truth, then, we view our life events as vital experiences making us wiser, kinder, deeper, and more compassionate. Believing that the world is our classroom we, then, can look for the lesson when:

- We receive diagnosis of cancer or other life-threatening illness;
- We are seriously injured;
- We lose a valued relationship;
- We experience the death of someone we love;
- We are betrayed by a friend;
- We discriminated against;
- We are forced to declare bankruptcy;
- We are misunderstood and persecuted;
- We are downsized and become unemployed;
- We discover a partner has been unfaithful;
- We are incarcerated.

The next time you receive bad news or are mistreated or become troubled by an issue recall Joanna Macy's wisdom: *The world itself has a role to play in our liberation Its very pressures, pains and risks can wake us up-release us from the bonds of ego and guide us home to our vast, true nature.* The world is our classroom. Though we cannot undo what has been done, we can learn from it and fast-forward our growth and evolution.

X

XENAGOGUE

GUIDING OTHERS TO GOODNESS

> To give one's self, to leave the world
> a bit better, whether by a healthy child,
> a garden patch or a redeemed social condition
> to know that even one life has breathed easier
> because you have lived this is to have succeeded.
> **Ralph Waldo Emerson**

The word *xenagogue* isn't in most people's vocabulary. Yet, if you've ever been guided along or led to a better place in your life, then you've encountered a *xenagogue*. The word is Greek in origin and simply means *to guide* or *to lead*. The term also implies *teacher* or *instructor*. Everyone who has some measure of light or enlightenment in their life ought to feel some responsibility to act a guide for others who are trailing behind. Consider this remarkable story told about Ryokan, a Zen Buddhist monk who lived in Japan 1758-1831. Though he was well known for his poetry and calligraphy, it was his kindness to all which made him a much loved and respected person.

One day, Ryokan heard his family complain that his nephew was wasting money on prostitutes. Family members challenged his behavior in many ways hoping he would change his ways but all to no avail. Upon hearing the family laments over this young man who seemed to be wasting his life and resources, Ryokan went to visit his nephew whom he had not seen for many years. His nephew invited him to stay one night. As was his custom, Ryokan spend the night sitting in meditation. As he was preparing to leave the next morning, he asked his nephew, "I must be getting old, my hand shakes so. Will you help me tie the string of my straw sandal?" The nephew helped him. Ryokan replied, "Thank you. A man gets older and feebler day by day. Take good care of yourself."

Then Ryokan left, without mentioning a word about prostitutes or the complaints of the family. But from that day on, his nephew truly reformed, and stopped spending money on prostitutes and began to live a more responsible life. This story shouts out the question: "What transpired?" Why did the young man turn his life around via a evening with his uncle Ryokan? Some possibilities include:

- Ryokan valued the youth enough to visit and simply be present without scolding, judging or pleading.
- Ryokan's request for the youth's assistance may have revealed to the young man that his life could be of service to others rather than just living for himself.
- Ryokan may have provided the youth with a badly needed role model of what it means to be a man.

As appealing as these possibilities may be, I suspect, however, that the main reason for the youth's remarkable transformation is this: *goodness is contagious.* Ryokan didn't have to say anything about the young man's life; he simply needed to be present. It was Ryokan's innate, powerful and contagious goodness which impacted and may have saved the life of his nephew.

For us there is this vital lesson: we must never underestimate the power we have to influence others. Let your light shine. Gladly take on the role of xenagogue - a spiritual guide for those you come in contact with. Allow your goodness to spill over and empower others to be good, noble, honorable, compassionate.

XENOPHILIA

THE PLANET NEEDS MORE XENOPHILIACS

> *We have enough religion to make us hate,*
> *but not enough to make us love one another.*
> **Jonathan Swift**, 1706

What our distressed planet needs are xenophiliacs. A xenophile is one who loves and appreciates people who are different. The term comes from two Greek words: *xenos* (a stranger, foreigner or something unknown) and *philos* (love). Put together the word literally means "love of the stranger". It's the complete opposite of xenophobia, those who dislike and even hate people who are different than themselves.

Consider the above quote from Jonathan Swift. It's deeply troubling because of its truth. Even in the early 18th century author Jonathan Swift observed the dark side of religion. Today, in the early 21st century the truth of his observation can be seen in world-wide conflicts: Muslims and Jews in the Middle East; Catholics and Protestants in Northern Ireland; Eastern Orthodox and Roman Catholics in various parts of Eastern Europe. There's just enough religion to make people hate but not enough to make them love one another. Of course, it doesn't have to be that way. If even a few people who adhere to a religion would practice what their faith teaches, it could make all the difference in the world. Some inspiring teachings from the religions which generate the most conflict today include:

* From Judaism: "What does the Lord require of you.to act justly, to love mercy and to walk humbly with your God." (Micah 6:8, Hebrew bible)

* From Christianity: "Love your enemies and bless those who persecute you." (Matthew 5:43) Also, "Love one another." (John 13:34) Both quotes are those of Jesus.

* From Islam: "A true Muslim is one who does not defame or abuse others; but the truly righteous becomes a refuge for humankind, their lives and properties." (The prophet Muhammad)

For planet earth to be a safer and more hospitable place, it needs more xenophiliacs. That's the essence of true religion. The Chinese sage, Confucius taught: "Is there any one maxim which out to be acted upon throughout one's whole life? Surely the maxim of loving kindness is such."

XMAS

MERRY PANCHA GANAPATI

> Peace and love are always alive in us,
> but we are not always alive to peace and love.
> **Julian of Norwich**

It may seem odd to include Xmas (Christmas) as an entry in a book about Eastern spirituality but here's the connection. One of the world's newest holidays was created by Satguru Sivaya Subramunayaswami, founder of the magazine *Hinduism Today.* In 1985 he proposed an alternative December holiday for western Hindu families. It is called *pancha ganapati,* a modern five-day festival observed from the 21st through 25th of December. Pancha (five) denotes Ganesha's (the Hindu elephant deity) five faces, each representing a specific power (shakti). One face is worshiped each day in the following manner:

- Day 1 is devoted to creating a vibration of love and harmony among immediate family members. Gifts are exchanged and placed unopened before a shrine or picture of Ganesha.
- Day 2 is devoted to creating a vibration of love and harmony among neighbors, relatives and close friends and presenting them with heartfelt gifts.
- Day 3 is devoted to creating a vibration of love and harmony among work colleagues and others who provide goods and services. Gifts are given.
- Day 4 is devoted to creating a vibration of love and appreciation for cultural arts. Various artistic gifts - art, music, dance, etc - are acknowledged and celebrated.
- Day 5 is devoted to deepening love consciousness. Family gifts given on the first day are now opened.

The festival has become a world-wide favorite among Hindu children and families. During these five days, cards are exchanged and communal meals enjoyed. It is a time of sharing gifts, renewing ties of family and friendship as well as focusing inward on God's generous blessings upon people. For those who object to the blatant materialism and commercialism connected to Christmas, perhaps some element of this Christian holiday can be helped to recover its spiritual roots by incorporating aspects of *Pancha Ganapati.*

XRAY

SEEING A BUDDHA IN ALL OTHERS

Skillful farmers don't throw away their manure.

They use it.
Lankavatara Sutra

One evening Shichiri Kojun (1836-1900) was meditating when a thief with a sharp sword entered, demanding wither his money or his life. Completely unfazed, Shichiri responded: "Do not disturb me. You can find the money in that drawer." Then he resumed his evening meditation practice. A few moments later, he interrupted meditation instructing the thief: "Don't take it all. I need some to pay taxes with tomorrow."

The intruder continue gathering up most of the money and started to leave. Again, Shichiri spoke: "You should thank a person when you receive a gift." The man thanked him and left.

A few days afterwards the man was caught and confessed to stealing not only from Shichiri but others in the neighborhood. Shichiri was called to court as a witness but surprised everyone when he said: "This man is no thief, at least as far as I am concerned. I gave him the money and he thanked me for it."

Because there were other witnesses and more evidence, the man was found guilty and sent to prison. After he had finished his prison term, the man went to Shichiri and became his disciple.

This story is well known and well liked in zen lore. It is generally titled "The Thief Who Became A Disciple." It is simply the story of a man converted or transformed because of the deep impression left upon him by the saintly man. This story is a powerful reminder for all of us to see the Buddha in every person we encounter no matter how difficult, how different, how obstinate, how unlovable the other person may be. Seeing the Buddha in him or her requires spiritual Xray vision which allows us to see beyond the external.

Skillful farmers don't throw away their manure. They use it . . . is the wisdom of the Lakavatara Sutra*. This applies greatly toward the people we encounter. We must train and strain our eyes to see the Buddha in everyone. No life should be allowed to be wasted.

Finally, before leaving this story, take a careful look at the two people involved because they both bring important life lessons for us all. Consider, first, Shichiri, who has these commendable virtues: he is unconcerned about his money; he exhibits no fear of the burglar; he remains calm, cool, composed in the presence of something which could be frightening and even dangerous. We can and should ask ourselves "how does one become like this?" and then follow the same path. Now, consider the burglar. To his credit he recognized the light which was presented itself to him _and_ he walked toward it rather than away from it. This man could have ignored the light which came his way and continued his life of imprisonment and crime. He came to a fork in the road of his life, one leading to more darkness and the other leading to light. Wisely, he chose to follow the light. Again, think about your life. When two options appear: positive or negative, good or less good; light or darkness; what road do you travel on?

(* According to tradition, the Lakavatara Sutra records the actual words of the Buddha as he entered Sri Lanka (formerly called Ceylon) and conversed with another enlightened teacher named Mahamati. This sutra figured prominently in the development of Chinese and Japanese Buddhism)

Y

YAMAS

AVOIDING SUFFERING

> If you feel "burnout" setting in, if you feel demoralized and
> exhausted, it is best, for the sake of everyone, to withdraw
> and restore yourself.
>
> **Dalai Lama**

One of India's greatest spiritual teachers was Patanjali.
Scholars estimate that Patanjali lived some times between
400 BCE and 200 AD, though they are in disagreement about
these dates. He was a spiritual genius whose books on yoga,
medicine and linguists are Hindu classics. Among his many
contributions to eastern spiritual philosophy are a famous
listing of ten commitments. The first five are called "Yamas"
and they advise avoiding behaviors which produce suffering.
The other five are called "Niyamas" and they advise
embracing behaviors which lead to happiness and fulfillment.
(Note: Turn back to the "N" section to read the Niyamas).
Here are Patanjali's yamas five activities which reduce
suffering:

1. *Ahmisa.* This literally means nonviolence and is the
concept utilized by Mahatama Gandhi and his movement
liberating India from British domination. Ahimsa reminds us
to relinquish hostility, anger, aggression and irritability.

2. *Satya.* Be truthful and honest in word and deed. It also
means being careful not to confuse our point of view with the
Truth.

3. *Asteya.* Don't take what isn't rightfully yours. It addresses theft recognizing there are many ways for us to steal. We can steal someone's time if we're chronically late. We can steal someone's energy if we are emotional vampires always living in a state of drama sucking others into our issues. We can steal someone's happiness by criticizing their achievements, etc.

4. *Brahmacharya.* Energy moderation or self control. The word literally means "walking in the way of God." Like the divine, we are not to permit our senses to rule nor are we to be urge driven. This applies to everything from how much we eat to how much we buy.

5. *Aparigraha* means "non grasping". It's about the decision not to hoard or accumulate goods through greed. Aparigraha challenges us to ask ourselves: "Before I buy this, do I really need it?" The problem with having too much of anything is that we can easily become attached to the stuff.
Review the five yamas from the perspective of your life. Which one(s) do you need to work on right now?

YAMMER   LEARNING TO QUIT COMPLAINING

> *If something can be changed, work to change it.*
> *If it cannot, why worry, be upset, and complain?*
> **Shantideva**

Yammer – to complain peevishly or whimperingly; to utter or say in a complaining or clamorous tone. (The American Heritage Dictionary)

A wealthy and aging merchant in ancient China experienced a series of catastrophic events. In rapid succession he lost his beautiful (but high maintenance wife), his estate to a fire, his fortune to embezzlement, and finally, he was incarcerated for offending the local governor.

A woman worked at the prison delivering food supplies. Previously she was employed by the formerly wealthy merchant. She noticed a change in the man who caught her attention. Formerly, he was known for being miserly, fearful and given to a great deal of complaining about the state of his life. But now, in prison, he seemed to be completely the opposite: calm, relaxed, peaceful and even happy. The woman wondered if he was in his right mind and asked him directly: "Why do you smile so much, laugh so easily and spend your days so pleasantly?" With a broad smile he answered: "I no longer have anything to lose."

That story has at these three powerful lessons in it. First, the man has finally dropped his attachments and carvings to things. The result: peace of mind *even in prison!* Secondly, he was no longer yammering – complaining – even though his circumstances are far less than ideal. Perhaps he was applying the wisdom of Shantideva's words: "If something can be changed, work to change it. If it cannot, why worry, be upset, and complain?" Thirdly, the man has made skillful use of his time. While incarcerated, he could simply "do" time or kill time or waste time. Instead, he used this time to reflect on life and what is important. Ironically, prison was the vehicle brought him these gifts.

Apply any of those lessons to your life. Perhaps you are a person who needs to stop yammering. Today, why not look to see what can be changed and work to change it. If it cannot be changed why complain? Secondly, look at the way you use your time. Are you wasting it, killing it off or are you skillfully using the precious seconds, minutes, hours, days, weeks and years that are allotted to you? Finally, have an honest look at yourself asking: "What are my attachments and cravings? What steps can I take to loosen my grip on them?"

YES

SAYING 'YES' TO YOUR DIVINE SELF

> We carry within us the wonders we seek without us.
> **Thomas Browne**

In ancient India lived a sculptor whose claim to fame resulted from his life-sized statues of elephants. People were impressed by his creations of elephants with trunks curled high, tusks thrust forward, thick legs, and an enormous body. Even more impressive was the fact he carved these huge creatures out of a single gigantic piece of granite.

Among the many who came to observe the sculptor at his place of work was a king who asked: "What is the secret of your artistry?" The sculptor explained: "With the assistance of many laborers, I cut a gigantic piece of granite from the banks of the river. Then I have it carefully brought here where it is set in my courtyard. For a long time I do nothing but observe this block of stone, studying it from every angle. Initially, I see nothing but a shapeless rock sitting there, perhaps resentful it has been separated from its home. Then, very, very slowly, I begin to detect something about the rock. A scarcely discernible outline begins to emerge revealing itself to me. As the outline grows stronger I see it! An elephant is stirring in there! Then, using my chisel and mallet, I chip away all of the unnecessary parts - all the parts which are not the elephant - until finally the elephant is freed."

This explanation is an excellent image for saying 'yes' to our divine self. Within each one of us is a spark of divinity. Out life task is to become attentive and aware of this true Self. Then, all that is required of ourselves is that we chip away whatever is not the divine in ourselves. By removing all that is petty, self-seeking, arrogant, and ignorant we will free and release our inner divinity.

What is it you need to chip away at in your life for this to happen?

Z

ZEAL

PRACTICING ZEALOUS PATIENCE?

> Patience plus zeal produces results.
> **Victor M. Parachin**

The Buddha's aunt, Prajapati, raised him after the death of his mother, Maya. She became his step-mother. Prajapati played a pivotal role on behalf of women in Buddhism. Even though the Buddha became an enlightened being who taught all, Buddhism was subject to the patriarchal influences of the day. Initially, the Buddha limited adherents of his philosophy to men. In his defense, he had to do this in order to ensure his teachings would be taken seriously and that his closest followers would not rebel.

However, Buddha's aunt Prajapati, took his teachings seriously. Encouraged by the Buddha's teaching that all sentient beings are equally valuable she approached him to defy the custom of the day and make his spiritual teachings available to both genders. She approached the Buddha three separate times about this matter reminding him of his own teachings. Each time the Buddha responded vaguely: "Do not set your heart on this."

Not one to give up easily, she appealed to the Buddha's closest companion and disciple, Ananda for assistance. Ananda approached Buddha on her behalf. Finally, the Buddha had to agree that a woman was just as capable of becoming enlightened as a man so he granted Prajapati the right to start an order of nuns. However, the Buddha was unable to completely distance himself from the patriarchal structure of his society. When he authorized Prajapati to establish her order of women he made it clear that the order of monks outranked the order of nuns. Nevertheless, Prajapati's efforts made it possible for Buddhism to be more open to women than other religions of the time.

There's an important lesson from this woman: patience plus zeal produces results. Prajapati did not give up. She approached the Buddha three separate times. When that failed, she spoke to the second in command of the movement. This took a patience built on zeal, which is another word for commitment. Prajapati understood the rightness of her cause and advanced it via her zealous patience. There's also an important lesson for us in this and it is this: *when we encounter resistance we must practice zealous patience.*

ZEN

DISMANTLING ANGER

> Anger dwells only in the bosom of fools.
> **A. Einstein**

In the Zen Buddhist tradition teachers are fond of telling stories to drive home a moral or spiritual lesson. Usually these stories come from ancient times. However, Zen teachers Leonard Scheff and Susan Edmiston tell this contemporary story which all of us can relate to. You are at the grand opening of a new mall which was built on the edge of town, where country meets city. For several minutes, you've been driving up and down the lanes looking for a parking spot. At last, you see the backup lights of a vehicle about to pull out. You stop, put on your turn signal and wait for the car to back out.

Suddenly from the other direction, a large SUV comes down the lane and pulls into the very spot you've been waiting for. Frustrated, you honk your horn but the driver gets out of the care, makes an obscene gesture at you and walks into the mall. The emotion you have is clear: you are angry!

Now, Scheff and Edmiston suggest changing the scene slightly. Instead of an SUV pulling into the spot, it is a cow which walks into the space from the other direction and settles down in the middle of it. (Remember, the new mall is on the edge of town) When you honk all she does is look up and moo but does not budge. What is your emotional response? Most likely it is amusement and not anger.

That story is a profound one and it's easy to miss the point. Here is what it's _not_ about: it's not about the driver of the SUV; it's not about the cow. It's all about us. The question raised by that story is this: what is the difference in those two scenes? On the one hand, there is no difference because the outcome is exactly the same – you need to find a different place to park. What is different, however, is your reaction. The story makes this point: we have a choice about anger. When faced with a disappointing or frustrating situation, we have response options. Unfortunately, for far too many people the first responder is always anger. This story reminds us it does not have to be that way. We do not have to limit ourselves to anger. We can consider other responses.

ZENCHISHIKI

WHO ARE YOUR TRAVELING COMPANIONS?

Even a feeble person will not stumble if those supporting him are strong, but a person of considerable strength, when alone, may lose his footing on an uneven path.

Ananda, the Buddha's closest companion and successor after his death, once asked Gautama: "It seems to me that by having good friends and advancing together with them, one has already halfway attained the Buddha way. Is this way of thinking correct?"

Buddha replied: "Ananda, this way of thinking is _not_ correct. Having good friends and advancing together with them is not half the Buddhist way but all the Buddhist way."

That answer may be surprising to some whose view of Buddhism is that of a solitary practice: silence, meditation, time away from the world. However, the Buddha exhibits wisdom in his answer because the people closest to us influence us greatly. Modern Buddhist teacher Daisaku Ikeda says: "Having good friends is like being equipped with a powerful auxiliary engine. When we encounter a steep hill or obstacle, we can encourage each other and fin the strength to keep pressing forward. Spiritual friends encourage us to continue soul growth and evolution. They uplift spiritual goals and ideals. Secular friends promote material objectives: money, work, success, pleasure, achievement, competition." The Buddha was reminding Ananda that se need to be with people who are our traveling companions as we journey on a spiritual path. This concept is so important that Buddhism has a term for it - **_Zenchishiki_** - which means a spiritual friend, someone who helps strengthen our faith and practice. We can find spiritual friends by participating in a mediation group, yoga class, or a church, synagogue, temple.

Ultimately, whether the friends we have are good or bad influences in our lives is entirely up to us. _Who are your traveling companions?_

ZOETIC

DISCOVERING THAT LESS IS MORE

> You're alive. That's good.
> Lower the bar!
> **John Tarrant**

The word zoetic is an uncommon English word which means "pertaining to life" and implies living which is vital and thriving. Perhaps there have been times in your life when you felt incredibly alive, happy and thriving. At that time you could have described yourself as "zoetic".

However, many people could not be described that way. They feel they are simply stumbling and struggling through life. Yet, the quote by John Tarrant is well worth reflection upon: "You're alive. That's good. Lower the bar!" To live a life which is rich with meaning, lowering the bar is an excellent idea. Often our expectations are far too high. We want the best of everything.

the best relationship,
the best family,
the best job,
the best education,
the best friends,
the best house,
the best schools,
the best neighborhood, etc.

Then when life does not produce our ideal we become disappointed and, sometimes, even despairing. When things don't work out the way we want them to in our lives, it's worth reminding ourselves: "You're alive. That's good. Lower the bar."

When we do that, positive energies are activated and we are able to respond with an openness and creativity to life as it unfolds. Consider the example of George Takei, a television actor who appeared in many programs including the *Start Trek* series. He was born into a Japanese American family. During World War II he grew up in internment camps surrounded by barbed wire and machines. "A searchlight followed us on night runs to the latrine. After the war my parents couldn't find housing and I had a teacher who called me 'little Jap boy' ", he recalls. In spite of injustice and harsh treatment, Takei forgave all. "My parents taught me that being bitter only pickles the one that stews in the brig." He found forgiving others to be personally "liberating." Rather than lament the state of his life, Takei said, in effect, "You're alive. That's good. Lower the bar!" In so doing, he went on to have an unusually successful career as an actor.

Perhaps today, if you are feeling discouraged about your life, offer yourself this reminder: "You're alive. That's good. Now, lower the bar!" That way you can gently nudge yourself from dismay and depression to a zoetic life.

INDEX

Made in the USA
Charleston, SC
06 December 2015